# Happiness for Beginners

*The Life Project of Feeling Good*

# Table of Content


**Manuscript 1** ...................................................................... 1

**Introduction** ..................................................................... 2

**Chapter 1:  What Is Stress?**...................................... 3

    *Stress on Your Body* ..................................................... 8

**Chapter 2:  What is Clutter?** .................................12

**Chapter 3:  Causes of Mental Clutter** ...................... 14

    Mental Clutter ................................................................15

**Chapter 4:  Symptoms of Clutter** .............................17

**Chapter 5:  Clutter and its Impact on Life**.................20

    The Effect of Clutter on the Brain ................................. 21

    Clutter Is Not Merely Physical.......................................22

**Chapter 6:  Declutter your mind and manage stress.** 24

    The Power of Stress Management.....................................24

**Chapter 7:  How to Reframe Negative Thoughts** ....... 32

    Question your thoughts. ...................................................33

    Replace negativity with positivity. ...................................34

    Refrain from turning molehills into mountains. ...............35

    Release your negative thoughts and talk about them.......35

    Go to the gym for a quick workout session. .....................36

    Do not allow your negative thoughts to bring you down. 37

    Aim to help other people achieve positivity in their lives. 37

Neuro-Linguistic Programming................................38

Disassociation.....................................................40

Content Reframing ..............................................41

Self-Anchoring ...................................................42

Rapport..............................................................43

Changing Beliefs ................................................44


## Chapter 8:  Choosing to Live Without Negativity ..... 48


Perceive your negative thinking patterns ........................49

Move away from negative thinkers................................49

Wind up noticeably mindful .....................................50

Pick constructive thoughts over destructive thoughts......51


## Chapter 9:  Why Declutter Your Mind .......................52


Being Efficient.....................................................53

Vicious Circle.......................................................53

Stop. Take a Step Back. Unclutter Your Mind. .................54


## Chapter 10:  How Minds Get Cluttered?....................56


Simplifying Your Life to achieve happiness .....................58


## Chapter 11:  Types of Mental Clutter ...................... 60

## Chapter 12:  Maintaining a decluttered mind............65


Stay away from unnecessary stress................................65

Modify the situation..............................................66

Adjust to the stressor ...........................................67

Acknowledge the things you can't change.....................68


## Chapter 13:  Decluttering your thoughts ...................70


Daily Stress .......................................................70

The Paradox of Choice...........................................70

Too Much "Stuff." ...............................................71

The Negativity Bias.................................................................72

Meditation ...............................................................................73

Set a clock for 10 minutes...................................................75

**Chapter 14: Importance of Decluttering Distractions that Cause Stress and Anxiety ...................................... 78**

Eliminating the Distraction................................................78

**Chapter 15: Investing in Yourself ............................... 81**

What is investing in yourself? .........................................81

Take in another ability. ......................................................83

Get over an old hindrance. ...............................................83

Make sound propensities.................................................84

Offer yourself a reprieve...................................................84

Instructions to Achieve What You Want in Life ...........85

Be consistent with your wants........................................86

Never stop. Affirm and visualize. ..................................87

The Golden Rule...................................................................88

Minimalist Living .................................................................89

Less is more...........................................................................90

Make space for what's vital .............................................91

More flexibility .....................................................................91

Concentrate on wellbeing and pastimes ....................92

Concentrate Less on material belonging ....................93

More joy...................................................................................94

Less dread of disappointment........................................95

More Certainty......................................................................95

Keep, toss, offer, give.........................................................96

Discover your direction .....................................................97

**Conclusion....................................................................99**

**Manuscript 2................................................................100**

**Introduction**....................................................................... **101**

**Chapter 1:  Happiness and success** .......................**102**

What is happiness?............................................104

Make yourself happy .........................................107

**Chapter 2: The Happiness advantage** ...................**109**

Happiness Benefits ...........................................110

**Chapter 3:  Characteristics of happy people**............**116**

Optimism .........................................................118

Seeing challenges not threats ..........................121

Social connections ...........................................127

**Chapter 4:  Be happy by choice not chance** .............**131**

What strategies should you choose? ................133

All you need is love ..........................................134

Gratitude .........................................................138

Journaling ........................................................141

Exercise............................................................145

Meditate and be mindful...................................147

Perform acts of kindness ..................................151

Your happiness shopping list.............................154

**Conclusion** ....................................................... **178**

# Manuscript 1

# Feeling Good

–––––– ❧❧❧ ––––––

## *Declutter Your Mind and Say Goodbye to Stress Forever*

## Chloe S

# Introduction

I want to thank you and congratulate you on purchasing the book, *"Feeling Good: Declutter Your Mind and Say Goodbye to Stress Forever"*

This book contains proven steps and strategies on how to achieve happiness especially to those people live the unhappy life and struggle in their life with too much messy stuff surrounding them and they are ready to change their lives completely by following this guide.

This simple guide offers the solution to happiness and the action plan to motivate your inner mind to forgive, forget and let go of the past

Many guides are going to provide advice and suggestions on what you can do declutter your mind, fix your immediate pain and overcome stress, but many of them just too hard to follow for the long term. In this book, you will learn several ways to decluttering your mind in step by step manner, and my advice to you is that you read through it and act immediately. I am sure it will help transform your life completely.

Thanks again for purchasing this book, I hope you enjoy it!

# Chapter 1:
# What Is Stress?

What's so stressful about a few chocolate chip cookies? Nothing, if you eat two chocolate chip cookies every day as part of a well-balanced diet. Plenty, if you deprive yourself of desserts for a month, then eat an entire bag of double fudge chocolate chunk. You aren't used to all those cookies. Your body isn't used to all that sugar. That's stressful. Not stressful like totaling your car or getting transferred to Siberia, but stressful nonetheless.

According to the American Institute of Stress in Yonkers, New York, 43 percent of all adults suffer adverse health effects due to stress, and 75 percent to 90 percent of all visits to primary care physicians are for stress-related complaints or disorders.

In the same way, anything out of the ordinary that happens to you is stressful on your body. Some of that stress feels good. Even great. Without any stress at all, life would be a big bore. Stress isn't, by definition, something bad, but it certainly isn't always good, either. In fact, it can cause dramatic health problems if it happens to you too much and for too long.

Stress isn't just out-of-the-ordinary stuff, however. Stress can also be hidden and deeply embedded in your life. What if you can't stand your job in middle management but continue to go there every day because you're afraid of starting your own business and giving up the regular paycheck? What if your family has serious communication problems, or if you live in a place where you don't feel safe? Maybe everything seems just fine, but nevertheless, you feel depressed. Even when you are accustomed to certain things in your life — dirty dishes in the sink, family members that don't help you out, twelve-hour days at the office — those things can be stressful. You might even get stressed out when something goes right. Maybe someone is helpful to you and you become suspicious, or you feel uncomfortable if your house is too clean. You are so used to things being difficult that you don't know how to adjust. Stress is a strange and highly individual phenomenon.

Unless you live in a cave without a television (actually, not a bad way to eliminate stress in your life), you've probably heard quite a bit about stress in the media, around the coffee machine at work, or in the magazines and newspapers, you read. Most people have a preconceived notion of what stress is in general, as well as what stress is to them. What does stress mean to you?

- Discomfort?

- Pain?

- Worry?

- Anxiety?

- Excitement?

- Fear?

- Uncertainty?

These things cause people to stress and are mostly conditions stemming from stress. But what is stress itself? Stress is such a broad term, and there are so many different kinds of stress affecting so many people in so many different ways that the word stress may seem to defy definition. What is stressful to one person might be exhilarating to another. So, what exactly is stress?

Stress comes in several guises, some more obvious than others. Some stress is acute, some are episodic, and some is chronic. Let's take a closer look at each kind of stress and how it affects you.

Stress Relief for Your Mind and Spirit

Stress management techniques that strengthen and reinforce the body will also help to strengthen the mind's ability to resist the negative effects of stress. But some stress management techniques directly deal with the mind — the thought processes, emotions, intellect, and, extending beyond the mind, the quest for spiritual meaning. In this chapter, we'll look at meditation techniques, which are the most effective techniques targeted to your mind and spirit.

The Negative Mental Effects of Stress

- An inability to concentrate

- Excessive, uncontrollable worrying

- Feelings of anxiety and panic

- Forgetfulness

- Sadness, depression

- Nervousness

- Fatigue, low energy

- Irritability

- Restlessness

- Negativism

- Fearfulness

- Unrealistic expectations

- Despair

Yes, some of these symptoms of stress can be directly connected to the body, but these symptoms are often a product of the mind and its interpretation of an obsession with or attachment to stressful events. How do you stress-proof your mind? With mental stress management, of course.

Stress management for the mind and the spirit is specifically targeted to help still, calm, and quiet the overactive mind, which is so common in people who are experiencing stress beyond their stress tolerance levels. These techniques help you to recognize the thought processes that are increasing your stress, the attitudes that can trigger a stress response, and the way you tend to cling to ideas as if they were life preservers. They can also fulfill the desire for higher meaning that, when thwarted by a life that isn't what we wanted it to be, can slowly erode our happiness and self-esteem.

Some of these techniques are related to physical stress management techniques (specifically, relaxation techniques) because, again, the mind and body are inextricably connected. But if you are experiencing even a few of the negative mental effects of stress or feel that your spirit is sorely in need of reinforcements and want to go straight to the source, try these stress management techniques for mind and spirit.

# Stress on Your Body

You can control some of the stresses on your body; for example, you can determine how much you eat and how much you exercise. These stresses fall into the physiological stressor category. Then, there are environmental stressors, such as environmental pollution and substance addiction.

1. **Environmental Stressors.** These are things in your immediate environment that put stress on your physical body. These include air pollution, polluted drinking water, noise pollution, artificial lighting, bad ventilation, or the presence of allergens in the field of ragweed outside your bedroom window or in the danger of the cat who likes to sleep on your pillow.

2. **Physiological stressors.** These are the stressors within your own body that cause stress. Bad health habits such as smoking, drinking too much, eating junk food, or being sedentary puts physiological stress on your body. So does illness, whether it's the common cold or something more serious like heart disease or cancer. The injury also puts stress on your body — a broken leg, a sprained wrist, and a slipped disk are all stressful.

One of the most common reactions to stress is compulsive eating. The best way to handle your temporary weakness is to find a healthier way to deal with your stressful feelings. A large glass of water, a walk around the block, or a phone call to a friend might be just what you need. Just remember, you can control your life.

Just as potent, but less direct, are stressors that impact your body by way of your mind. For example, getting caught in heavy traffic may stress your body directly because of the air pollution it creates, but it may also stress your body indirectly because you get so worked up and irritated sitting in your car in the middle of a traffic jam that your blood pressure rises, your muscles tense, and your heart beats faster. If you were to interpret the traffic jam differently — say, as an opportunity to relax and listen to your favorite CD before getting to work — your body might not experience any stress at all. Again, attitude plays a major role.

Pain is another, trickier example of indirect stress. If you have a terrible headache, your body may not experience direct physiological stress, but your emotional reaction to the pain might cause your body significant stress. People tend to be fearful of pain, but the pain is an important way to let us know something is wrong. Pain can signal injury or disease. However, sometimes we already know what's wrong. We get migraines or have arthritis, or experience menstrual cramps or a bad knee acts up when the weather changes. This kind of "familiar" pain isn't useful in terms of alerting us to something that needs immediate medical attention.

But because we know we are in some form of pain, we still tend to get tense. "Oh no, not another migraine! No, not today!" Our emotional reaction doesn't cause the pain, but it does cause the physiological stress associated with the pain. Pain in itself isn't stressful. Our reaction to pain is what causes stress. So, learning stress management techniques may not stop the pain, but it can stop the physiological stress associated with pain.

Therapies designed to help people manage chronic pain counsel patients to explore the difference between pain and the negative interpretation of pain. People living with chronic pain learn meditation techniques for entering and confronting pain apart from the brain's interpretation of the pain as a source of suffering.

When your body is experiencing this stress response, whether caused by direct or indirect physiological stressors, it undergoes some very specific changes. Around the beginning of the twentieth century, physiologist Walter B. Cannon coined the phrase "fight or flight" to describe the biochemical changes stress invokes in the body, preparing it to flee or confront danger more safely and effectively. These are the changes that happen in your body every time you feel stressed, even if running away or fighting aren't relevant or wouldn't help you (for example, if you're about to give a speech, take a test, or confront your mother-in-law about her constant unsolicited advice, neither fight nor flight is very helpful responses).

**Here's what happens inside your body when you feel stress:**

1. Your cerebral cortex sends an alarm message to your hypothalamus (the part of your brain that releases the chemicals that create the stress response.) Anything

your brain perceives as stress will cause this effect, whether you are in any real danger.

2. Your hypothalamus releases chemicals that stimulate your sympathetic nervous system to prepare for danger.

3. Your nervous system reacts by raising your heart rate, respiration rate, and blood pressure. Everything gets turned "up."

4. Your muscles tense, preparing for action. Blood moves away from the extremities and your digestive system, into your muscles and brain. Blood sugars are mobilized to travel to where they will be needed most.

5. Your senses get sharper. You can hear better, see better, smell better, taste better. Even your sense of touch becomes more sensitive.

# Chapter 2:
# What is Clutter?

Realize that you can vanquish anything and get anything you need. Why is it hard for some? All things considered, this is a direct result of a mental mess.

Mental perplexity is only musings, emotions, and tension that is bunched up in your mind and leads you into a condition of self-disrupt, enduring, battle, stress, and partition. Mental mess makes life hard and confused. The stuff puts us inconsistent with every other person. We can't see it, yet mental perplexity sneaks where peace and love don't. In the event that we are jumbled, we are opposing the regular stream and simplicity of life. We are not enabling ourselves to achieve our maximum capacity or finding our genuine implications.

Like I said earlier in the event that you hold a serious conviction of what you have is as of now there, at that point you will show it in your life. When you have a mental mess, it gets muddled; you will have excessively numerous considerations driving your psyche to head in a wide range of bearings. There is also possible a voice inside your head saying that it is all good for nothing. At that point, you have another voice in your mind saying that it is everything to you and that you ought to never surrender. Also, at last, the inquiry comes to which one to take after? Furthermore, noting this will be hard.

On the off chance that you are not encountering transparency, peace, and adore, you have a mental mess. It lives solely in your musings. What's more, it just takes one negative idea or feeling to misdirect you into a substantially more critical and ruinous life. Presently, there are eight standard indications of a mental mess.

# Chapter 3:
# Causes of Mental Clutter

Mental clutter is caused by a variety of factors. Before you learn about these factors, it is crucial to determine psychological confusion first.

In the story, there was a man who wanted to hang a painting on the wall. He had a nail, but he did not have a hammer. So, he thought of going to his neighbor's house to borrow a stick. However, he started to have doubts.

What if his neighbor refused to lend him his hammer? His neighbor barely spoke to him the day before. Perhaps, he was in a hurry. Maybe he had something against him. Why would he hold anything against him when he did not do anything wrong?

If his neighbor wanted to borrow something, he would readily lend it. So, why would he refuse to let him borrow a hammer? These types of people are the ones that make others miserable, he thought. Even worse, he might feel that he needed him because of the hammer.

With such thoughts, the man rushed to his neighbor's house and yelled mean things at him before his neighbor even had any idea of why he came to his door.

This story illustrates what a mentally cluttered person is like. Clutter is the junk that floats around in a mentally cluttered person's head. It is what causes him to jump to ridiculous and unreasonable conclusions.

# Mental Clutter

Mental clutter is the trash that you hoard in your mind. It can cause you to think of the worst. It can keep you pessimistic, fearful, and anxious, trapped in the web of your making. It can also get you stuck in self-sabotage, struggle, suffering, separation, and stress. It can make your life complicated and confusing. It can even put you at odds with everyone else.

Mental clutter is hidden from the naked eye. It also lurks in places where there is no love or peace. The longer you stay cluttered, the longer you resist the ease and flow of life.

If you do not experience peace, love, and clarity, your mind is cluttered. The mental clutter is elusive and exclusive in your thoughts. It begins as a head for, which is misleading and cloudy. Slowly but surely, it evolves into something bigger and worse.

Your mental clutter consists of stories that you tell yourself. These are the stories that cripple your potential and attack your wellbeing. It tells you that you cannot, should not, and will not. It gives you a reason to distrust and doubt, leaving you feeling helpless. It tells you of lies of lack and limitation instead of the truth regarding wealth and abundance.

When it accumulates and blinds you to the truth of who you are, without any limiting beliefs, you become the man who needed a hammer and who spiraled down the rabbit hole. You become a person who believes that he is not good enough, does not deserve to be loved, and will not have

what he wants. When you clear away this mess, the truth is
revealed.

# Chapter 4:
# Symptoms of Clutter

How can you tell if you already have too much clutter? There are eight telltale symptoms that you have to watch out for. When you notice these symptoms starting to show, you need to start decluttering.

## Confusion

This is the lack of understanding and clarity. It is uncertainty or being unclear about certain things. When you are confused, you feel scattered and out of sorts. It causes you to start being fearful and worried.

## Chatter

Chatter refers to the ongoing narrative at the back of your head. It is jibber jabber, noise, and inner dialogue. It feels like a constant mental dialogue that drones on in your background. It is impatient and curious.

## Chaos

This refers to the total disarray, disorder, disruption, and disorganization in your head. It leads to mental anarchy and feels like having no organization or order in spite of dissenting beliefs and ideas.

## Conditions

These are defined as stipulations, prerequisites, or requirements. They also refer to factors that influence outcomes or progressions of certain situations. They are the expectations and demands that people place on themselves and others. They can seem like boundaries, limits, and rules.

## Collections

These refer to the grouping or gathering of objects. They see to the stockpiling of security, comfort, and prestige. They can feel like validation and trophies of acknowledgment.

## Comparisons

These refer to the formation of superlative or comparative judgments. Comparison deliberately takes two things and pits them against each other to select a preference or winner. It can feel like searching for something better and more prominent.

## Commitments

These refer to the allocation of energy to different activities or causes within a particular timeframe. You commit to both action and attention to everything, including work, family, health, and hobbies. Commitments can feel like filling your calendar with obligations and appointments.

## Control

This refers to the power to influence behaviors or courses of events. Through it, you can seek to enslave the action and performance of your life so that you can get your desired results. It can feel like manipulating and managing circumstances to make you more comfortable.

# Chapter 5:
# Clutter and its Impact on Life

People collect things for different reasons. Some people think they will need to use those words later on or perhaps their future children would use them. Others collect items because they have an emotional attachment to them. After all, a lot of people like to keep things that have sentimental value. There are also those who feel like they would only be wasting money if they throw away their expensive things, no matter how old, broken, or useless they are already.

You may be holding on to a nice pair of shoes you have not worn in years because you believe there will come an occasion where you can wear them again. You may keep refusing to donate unread books that take up a lot of space in your room because you keep telling yourself there will come a time when you will finally read them. There are indeed lots of reasons why people hold onto their things.

The truth, however, is that you probably just made a mistake purchasing or acquiring those things in the first place. This can be difficult for your brain to process. Researchers at Yale University said that two areas of your mind are linked to pain. These are the insula and the anterior cingulate cortex. They light up as a response when you let go of things that you feel connected to.

Your anterior cingulate cortex is the same area of your brain that lights up whenever you experience physical pain. It views the loss of clutter as something that causes physical pain. This explains why the more you financially or emotionally commit to a thing, the stronger your desire gets to keep it.

Every time you introduce a new item into your life, you readily associate it with value. This makes it more difficult for you to give it up or let it go when it is time to do so. Because of your psychological connection to things, you start to accumulate more.

## The Effect of Clutter on the Brain

There is a misconception that hoarding things is not harming anyone. It hurts the hoarder. Hoarding is a severe obsessive-compulsive disorder that requires a long-term solution. It does not only affect the patient, but it also affects the people living with him as well as those who care about his wellbeing.

Having unnecessary things around can hurt your ability to process information and retain your focus. Your attachment to clutter can result in stress, depression, and embarrassment. It can also endanger your life if your hoarding goes out of control.

For example, if you fill your house with junk, you may no longer be able to move around, and you may be in danger of things falling on you. You may also have a hard time maintaining proper hygiene, causing you to develop infections and illnesses. Also, your house can be infested with rats and other pests because of all the garbage.

Neuroscientists at Princeton University have found that physical clutter tends to compete for attention. This causes increased stress and diminished performance. You will not be able to perform appropriately in an unorganized environment because the mess and clutter around you will keep you distracted.

Researchers at the University of California, Los Angeles (UCLA) did a study that involved several mothers as participants. At the end of it, they found that the stress hormones of all the participants spiked when they dealt with their personal belongings. Thus, it was concluded that physical clutter overloads the senses just as multitasking overwhelms the brain. As a result, you become more stressed out, and your ability to focus and think creatively diminishes when clutter surrounds you.

Peter Walsh, a well-known author, and host of reality television series Extreme Clutter said that things left undone might be your undoing. Clutter only adds stress and wastes valuable time. Unorganized individuals with cluttered lives tend to feel anxious, out of control, and frustrated. They often have a hard time relaxing and unwinding as well.

So, if you want to have more peace of mind, you need to declutter and organize your belongings and surroundings. Decluttering generates fresh energy, releases negative emotions, and creates physical and mental space.

## Clutter Is Not Merely Physical

Papers, carton boxes, bottles, plastic bags, broken appliances, and other material items are not the only clutter in your home. Even the files in your computer can be regarded as clutter. Digital clutter can be just as bad as physical clutter. When you have too many unnecessary files on your computer, you may be distracted. You may have a hard time focusing on work and completing tasks.

For example, if you have so many items on your to-do list, you may feel overwhelmed and get confused about what to do first. If you keep receiving notifications, your brain may not have a chance to process the experience entirely. In essence, if your mind has too much going on in it, its power decreases. This can give you a hard time filtering information, maintaining an active working memory, and quickly switch between tasks.

# Chapter 6:
# Declutter your mind and manage stress

What best mitigates weight is similarly personal. You may have endeavored some direct sounding conditions for managing your weight and found that they aren't that helpful.

## The Power of Stress Management

Stress organization tips are tied in with helping you develop a convincing weight organization system. Effective weight organization relies upon an attempted, careful approach that fuses both cognizances of stress and lifestyle changes.

The going with six clues are laid out by that.

### Tip 1: Identify affinities and practices that show weight

It's not hard to recognize wellsprings of stress following an imperative life event, for instance, advancing occupations, moving home, or losing a companion or relative, yet pinpointing the purposes behind common weight can be more trapped. It's extremely not by any means clear your considerations, notions, and practices that add to your sentiments of tension. Apparently, you may understand that you are, for the most part, worried overwork due dates, yet maybe it's you're postponing, rather than the certifiable movement asks for, that is causing the weight.

To recognize your correct wellsprings of stress, look at your inclinations, perspective, and reasons:

Do you clear up away criticalness as brief ("I just have a million things going on the present minute") in spite of the way that you can't recall the last time you chilled?

Do you portray stress as a fundamental bit of your work or home life ("Things are always crazy around here") or as a bit of your personality ("I have a lot of restless essentialness that is it more or less")?

Do you blame your stress for different people or outside events, or view it as inside and out normal and unexceptional?

Until the point that the moment that you recognize obligation with respect to the part you play in making or caring for it, your sentiment uneasiness will remain outside your control.

**Start your weight journal**

A weight journal can empower you to perceive the reliable stressors for the duration of your life and the way you oversee them. Each time you grab centered; make sure to screen it in your journal. The thing is this: as you keep a step by step log of these events, you will begin to see illustrations and normal themes with these stressors.

Thusly, record these things in your journal:

What caused your weight (figure in case you aren't sure?)

How might you feel, both physically and deep down?

How might you act on account of the stressor?

What did you move forward?

**Tip 2: Replace terrible adjusting techniques to sound ones**

By and by, consider the routes you are starting at now administer and adjust to stress in your life. Your weight journal can empower you to remember them. Are the adjusting frameworks you apply sound or terrible, strong or ineffectual? Heartbreakingly, people have a tendency to adjust to stress in ways that compound their worry.

There are tragic ways people have a tendency to adjust to weight. These adjusting frameworks may by chance diminish weight, in any case, they cause more mischief as time goes on:

Smoking

Using pills or meds to loosen up

Drinking substantially more than you should

Resting more than you should

Pigging out on so much junk or comfort support

Deferring your activities/commitments

Wandering off in fantasy land for an impressive period of time since you are looking at your phone

Finishing off every snapshot of the day since you are running from your issues

Pulling once more from colleagues, family, and activities and staring off into space

Taking out your weight on others out of disappointment

In case these systems you apply don't add to your more basic eager and physical prosperity, by then the open door has just traveled every which way to find more useful ones. No single approach works out for everyone neither in every situation, so certification to investigate distinctive roads with respect to various strategies and systems. Focus on what impacts you to feel calm and in charge of your case.

**Tip 3: Get moving and gain ground**

Unknowingly, physical activity accepts a massive vital part in diminishing and keeping the effects of weight, yet you don't have to be a contender nor put hours in a rec focus to experience the points of interest. Practically any kind of physical activity can enable straightforwardness to weight and expend with extreme warmth all the shock, strain, and frustration. Exercise tends to release endorphins that reason a lift in your perspective and impacts you to feel phenomenally right, and it can moreover fill in as a critical preoccupation to your step by step pushes.

Regularly, most extraordinary favorable circumstances rise up out of honing for 30 minutes or more, yet you can start pretty much nothing and build up your wellbeing level consistently. Short, 10-minute impacts of activity tend to lift your heart rate and impact you to break out into a sweat which supports you relieve weight and give you greater essentialness and optimism.

## Manage your stress with standard exercise

By and by, once you're in the inclination for being physically powerful, do endeavor to intertwine regular exercise into your entire step by step design. Activities that are diligent and cadenced—which require moving both your arms and your legs—are most especially practical at decreasing weight. Walking, running, swimming, jumping, cycling, tai - chi, and oxygen devouring classes are excellent choices.

Pick that one activity you acknowledge as this makes you more slanted to remain with it. While working out, try to focus on your body and all physical (and as a less than dependable rule excited) sensations you experience as you're moving and not on your contemplations. Adding this care segment to your action routine won't merely empower you to break out of the cycle of negative contemplations that often runs with overwhelming weight, however, helps move your essentialness, positive imperativeness, to the most centered around part of your body. While working out, consistently focus on sorting out your breathing with every advancement you make. For example, endeavor to perceive how the air or sunlight feels on your skin. Simply getting away from your head and concentrating on how you feel while doing these is the surest technique to refrain from getting harm and clean yourself up.

## Tip 4: Connect to people

Social engagement has been believed to be the speediest and most capable way to deal with, lessen and chop down a leg on push and go without going over the edge to inside or external events that are believed to incapacitate. Getting the chance to express what you're encountering can be to a great degree cathartic, paying little respect to whether it shows up there is nothing you can do to alter that particularly troubling situation. We, in general, know the slant having a calmed slant in the wake of talking with someone else who impacts us to feel shielded and got on. This specific experience of security—as observed and related to us by our tangible framework—occurs in light of nonverbal signs that begin from what we hear, see and feel.

The internal ear, face, heart, and stomach are wired together in such a course to the mind that social relationship with another person versus through looking, listening carefully, talking, et cetera can quickly calm you down and put the brakes on protected weight responses like "fight-or-flight." It furthermore releases hormones that move to diminish weight, paying little mind to whether you can't alter that particular unsavory situation itself. In all trustworthiness, it's not for the most part sensible to have a mate close by to slant toward, to talk when you feel overwhelmed by weight, yet it hints at change when you amass and keep up an arrangement of dear colleagues who will empower you to improve your flexibility to life's stressors. On the contrary side, the all the

29

more devastate and separated you are yourself, the higher you lack protection to weight.

Contact your family and friends and routinely relate up close and personal, and not through calls. The real thing here is that people you banter with don't need the ability to settle your weight; they basically ought to be right group of onlookers individuals to you. Opening up isn't an indication of weakness as you may think and it won't make you a weight to others. Honestly, most colleagues will be complimented that you trust them okay to confide in them about what you are experiencing, and it won't simply fortify your cooperation bond yet what's more upgrade your success. Likewise, remember, it's never past the point where it is conceivable to develop new fellowships and strengthen your empowering gathering of individuals paying little heed to whether you figure your mien towards people can never hint at change.

## Tip 5: Try and put aside a couple of minutes for excitement just and loosening up

When you go past an accept accountability approach and an elevating perspective, you can reduce stress in your life by means of individual out a touch of "individual" time. Make an effort not to get so compensated for lost time in the humming about of your life that you disregard to manage your own specific needs. Supporting yourself is a need you have to educate into your life, not an indulgence. If you frequently put aside a couple of minutes for excitement and loosening up, you will easily have the ability to manage life's stressors as you have a better limit successfully than loosen up when you feel centered.

Set aside a particular time to loosen up. Fuse "Bona fide" rest in your step by step design. "Authentic" here induces not loosening up with clearing bills what not. Do whatever it takes not to empower distinctive duties regarding assault starting at now.

# Chapter 7: How to Reframe Negative Thoughts

Negative thoughts can drag you down and leave you paralyzed with anxiety or depression. They make you feel demotivated and discouraged. They make you walk around with a rain cloud over your head all the time. If you continue to harbor negative thoughts, you will hold yourself back and prevent yourself from living life the way you want to.

The best way to overcome your negative thoughts is to make an effort to change the way you think. When you change your mindset, you will be able to change your behavior. The following tips are effective in helping people overcome their negative thoughts and replace them with more positive ones: Find what is helpful or good when you find yourself in a seemingly negative situation.

Everybody, including the most successful people in the world, experiences setbacks, and failures. When you do not get what you want, you may feel negative emotions and cause you to see things in a negative manner. When this happens, you have to counter it by asking certain questions. These questions should help you feel better as well as help you grow.

For example, you can ask yourself what good thing you can see in the situation or what you can do differently in case you find yourself in the same situation in the future. You can also ask yourself about the lesson that you have learned from the experience. Furthermore, you can put yourself in the shoes of other people. What do you think your friends will tell you or advise you to do to effectively deal with the situation you are in.

Remind yourself that other people do not really care about what you do or say.

You may end up with negative thoughts when you start thinking that other people may think or say something about you. This causes you to over analyze things to the point of no longer being rational. If you continue to do this, you will soon lose touch of reality and get caught up in your negative thoughts.

You have to realize that people do not really have a lot of energy or time to talk about you or think about the things you do. In fact, they are too consumed with their own lives, which include issues with their jobs, children, finances, *etc.* They have their own worries and fears, so they will not think twice about yours.

If you remind yourself of this truth, you will be set free from constraints. You will be able to take the necessary steps to reach your own goals and live your life the way you have always wanted to.

## Question your thoughts.

Every time you catch yourself having negative thoughts, you should start questioning them. Ask yourself if you have to take the negative thought seriously or play with it. The answer is most likely a 'no'. You can lighten up your situation by playing or challenging your negative thoughts to lessen their impact.

You also have to analyze the situation. Find out why you came up with negative thoughts in the first place. The root causes can vary. You may be hungry, tired, or even bored. Whatever the reason is, you have to deal with it accordingly.

When you question your negative thoughts, you make yourself grounded. You become levelheaded and you gain a more sensible perspective. You realize that experiencing negativity does not erase the fact that positivity still exists.

## Replace negativity with positivity.

Look around you. What do you see? What do you allow inside your mind? Whatever your answer is, it has a huge effect on your life. Thus, you have to be mindful of the thoughts that you allow inside your mind.

Question yourself regarding the top three negativity sources you have. The answer may pertain to people, music, social media, *etc.* Then, you have to question yourself about what you can do to lessen the amount of time you spend on these negativity sources.

Make it a point to follow up on this. Spend less time on your negativity sources and more time on your positivity sources. It is always a better idea to go with the positive.

# Refrain from turning molehills into mountains.

To prevent negative thoughts from growing inside your mind, you have to confront them as soon as possible. Do not allow negative things to get worse. You can zoom out of them by asking yourself if your current problems are still going to matter several weeks, months, or years from now. You will realize that they are really just nothing. Refrain from turning such molehills of negativity into mountains of negativity.

# Release your negative thoughts and talk about them.

Sometimes, letting things out and talking them over is the best solution to a problem. If you keep your negative thoughts inside your mind, they will grow. Hence, you have to release them. You can talk to a friend or a therapist. Venting about the issues you have within you can help you unload the burden that you feel. It can also help you change your perspective about your situation and encourage you to search for feasible solutions or courses of action.

Live your life and then come back to the moment.

If you find yourself starting to harbor negative thoughts, you might be recalling a past event or anticipating a future one. Your moods can be confusing and your thoughts troubling.

To get rid of such thoughts, you have to fully focus on the present moment. Be mindful of whatever is happening to your right at that moment. When you focus on the present, you will be more open-minded and less likely to engage in negative thinking.

One way to encourage yourself to focus on your present moment is to focus on your breathing. Pause for a minute or two and then take deep breaths. When you inhale, the air should go in through your nose and fill up your belly. Then, it should go out through your mouth. As you repeatedly inhale and exhale, you have to focus on the air going in and out of your body alone. Do not think of anything else during this time.

Another ideal way how you can focus on your present moment is to observe your surroundings and focus on the things that you see. Take a break for one to two minutes, get your thoughts out of your mind, and then concentrate on the things that you see around you. You can also focus on the passers-by, the birds, the trees, the clouds, the warmth of the sun on your skin, the smell of the freshly baked bread, or even the traffic noise in the streets.

## Go to the gym for a quick workout session.

Exercise gives you endorphins, which are natural chemicals that can make you happier. Each time you feel down, you should exercise. If you have a hectic schedule and you cannot afford half an hour for a workout, you can simply do ten to fifteen minutes.

The important thing is that you did it. It does not matter how long you exercised, as long as you did it. In addition, working out helps you distract yourself from your negative thoughts. It helps you attain focus and may even encourage you to harbor positive thoughts.

## Do not allow your negative thoughts to bring you down.

A lot of people make the mistake of letting their fears get the best of them. If you are one of these people, you may choose to run away from your issues instead of facing them. You may have the impulse to avoid your fears, but you have to understand that they can get worse if you do not deal with them properly.

One way to deal with a situation like this is to ask yourself about the worst possible case that can happen. Eventually, you will realize that the worst-case scenario is not that bad. You will also be prompted to take action and reduce the possibility of it actually occurring. When you do this, you will have clarity and your fear will be lessened.

## Aim to help other people achieve positivity in their lives.

If you allow yourself to be stuck with your negative thinking patterns, you will not improve and grow as a person. Thus, you have to get out of your head. Do not let yourself have a victim mindset. Redirect your energy into positivity. Aim to help others. When you do this, you will feel better as well as become more optimistic. You can help another person gain positivity in their life by being kind, listening to them, and saying good things about them. It is important to be genuine.

Practice gratitude and be thankful for everything that you have.

When you become grateful for the little things that you have, you become more appreciative of the bigger things that you receive. You also open yourself up for more blessings. Oftentimes, people get so caught up in their day to day lives that they forget to appreciate the wonderful things they have around them.

Each morning make an effort to notice the blessings that you have such as sunlight, water, food, air, *etc.* You tend to neglect these things because you are used to having them on a daily basis. Imagine your life without them and you would be surprised by how much you actually need them. When you become grateful for your blessings, you receive more good things.

## Neuro-Linguistic Programming

Neuro-Linguistic Programming (NLP) involves neurology, language, and programming – the three most influential components that produce human experience. It is an epistemology or a pragmatic school of thought that addresses issues associated with human nature.

It focuses on two presuppositions: life and mind are systematic processes, which means that your body, the universe, and societies all form complex systems and subsystems that mutually influence and interact with one another; and the map is not the territory, which means that you can have your own perception of reality but cannot really know it because you are only human.

NLP offers ways on how you can alter your thinking patterns. It can help you change how you think, approach your life, and view events from your past. It is efficient and practical. It can help you control your mind and your life in general. However, unlike psychoanalysis, it does not focus on 'why' but rather on 'how'.

The main principle behind NLP is that even though you cannot control every aspect of your life, you can still control the way you think and act towards various situations. Certain external factors are out of your control, such as accidents, death, and failed relationships. It is up to you how you will perceive them. It is really what goes on in your head that matters.

Keep in mind that your feelings and thoughts are neither things that you *have* nor *are*, but rather what you *do*. Usually, their causes are complicated and may even involve beliefs or comments from other people. Through NLP, you can learn how to take control of these influences and beliefs. You can learn how to get over your greatest fears and phobias as well.

The following methods should be done in order to decrease mental clutter:

# Disassociation

Emotions can greatly affect one's actions. You can get angry, upset, or stressed out in an instant, causing you to do things without thinking them through. For example, when somebody upsets you, you may respond by saying hurtful words or getting revenge.

With NLP, you can learn how to neutralize your negative emotions by viewing situations in an objective manner. This allows you to be more reasonable.

To practice the technique of disassociation, you have to identify the emotion that you want to eliminate. This can be fear, uneasiness, or dislike of a certain person, object, event, or location.

Visualize yourself being in this situation from the very beginning. However, instead of viewing yourself as the main participant, you should view yourself as a mere observer.

Play the scenario backward and then fast forward and backward again in your head, as if you are watching a movie on the big screen. You can add music for a more dramatic effect. Choose something funny and light so that you will also feel lighter. Repeat this step three to four times more.

Next, visualize the event as something that occurs in the present. Notice your emotions towards the stimuli changing or disappearing. If you still have the same negative emotions as you did before, you should keep doing this exercise until your negative emotions completely vanish.

## Content Reframing

Whenever you find yourself stuck in a situation in which you feel angry or powerless, you can try content reframing. It can help you change how you perceive your current situation, so you can view it in a different frame or a more empowering way.

To help you understand content reframing better, consider this scenario: You have just been let go from work. You have no job. If you think about it, a lot of things can go wrong in this situation. You have no more source of income, so you will eventually drain your bank account. When you use up all your savings, you will not be able to pay rent, buy food, and commute. You will become homeless, be at risk of illnesses, or even starve to death.

Then again, you can also view the same situation in a different context. How can you do this? Rather than go with the negative outcome, you should go with the positive possibility.

Since you no longer have this job, you now have more time to focus on what you want as well as explore different areas of expertise. You can develop more skills and hone your talents. It can also be a learning opportunity. Through your mistakes, you can come up with better decisions and find ways on how to improve your work.

Having this kind of adversity can also make you stronger. You have experienced rock bottom, so you should now be more motivated to get back up. Ten years from now, you can look back at this experience and feel so much better because you have come a long way.

You can always reframe your content. You can change the way you view situations and take your focus away from the negativity. This allows you to view the situation in a completely different manner. When you focus on the positive, it becomes easier to come up with better and more reasonable decisions.

Refrain from panicking and thinking fear-based thoughts because this will only cause you to have deeper problems and more failures. Remember that every situation has both good and bad points. Instead of focusing on the bad, you should focus on the good.

## Self-Anchoring

In NLP, self-anchoring is used to obtain an emotional response to words said or actions done.

For example, people may smile unconsciously when you touch their shoulder. A girl may response in shock when you pull her hair. It is possible to instantaneously change the way you feel. When you are angry, upset, or insecure, don't worry because such negative feeling can quickly go away. You just have to anchor a positive emotional response to it and fire this anchor every time you start to feel the negative emotion.

Determine the state that you wish to experience, whether it is happiness, excitement, *etc.* Do everything you can to reach that particular state. Your body language can do wonders. Try sitting straight, smiling, or doing a power pose. You can also try recalling a happy memory.

Once you reach that state, visualize a smoke circle in front of you. Then, imagine yourself stepping into that circle and feeling great. Hold this visualization until you feel positive energy flow within your body.

Now, it is time to get out of the circle. Imagine yourself stepping outside and thinking of something else. The purpose of this is to have a different emotion. You should feel something else that is completely unrelated to your previous one.

After a while, imagine yourself going back inside the circle. Observe how you respond to this move. If you feel the same emotion as you did when you previously stepped inside the circle, then you know that the technique has worked.

## Rapport

It is important to build rapport with others. It is vital not only for succeeding in life but also for gaining peace of mind and getting rid of mental clutter.

You can follow the breathing patterns or mirror the body languages of other people. Try to be as natural as you can. You can also use the same words that they use. Make sure that you are discreet.

You can also assess their primary sensory perception, whether it is auditory or kinesthetic. Then, you can use that same perception yourself. You can pay attention to their choice of words or just talk to them.

You can tell that the primary sensory perception of a person is auditory if that person makes use of words or phrases such as "I am listening to you", "I hear you", or "She has a loud voice". It is actually easy to determine primary sensory perception. It is auditory if noise and sound are involved.

On the other hand, you can tell that the primary sensory perception of a person is visual if he uses words or phrases such as "You have a bright future", "My vision is very clear", or "I see what you mean". In essence, the primary sensory perception is visual if it involves darkness, brightness, glitter, or any other elements that can be seen.

A person has a kinesthetic primary sensory perception if he uses words or phrases such as "He has a pleasant vibe", "I do not feel right about this" or "I have a good feeling about this". The primary sensory perception is kinesthetic if it involves touch, warmth, coolness, or any other element that can be felt.

## Changing Beliefs

Whatever you believe in will eventually come true. This is what the Law of Attraction, one of the Universal laws, states. Whatever you constantly think about and whatever you believe with all your heart can eventually happen.

If you have positive beliefs, then you can see a bright future ahead of you. On the contrary, if you keep harboring negative and limiting beliefs, you can always experience mishaps and other misfortunate events.

There are three fundamental types of limiting beliefs, and these are beliefs about meaning, beliefs about the cause, and beliefs about identity. Each of these beliefs can influence the way you perceive the world. They can also affect the way you filter out parts of reality that do not fit with your belief system. It is actually your beliefs that let you experience awareness with regard to the different aspects of reality that harmonize with them.

Your beliefs are powerful since they can determine the experiences that you will have in your life. They are developed when you encounter something that relates to your experiences. For example, you may experience something bad or damaging. It is up to you how you will handle it.

You can either let it consume your entire being or learn from it and move on with your life. Whichever option you choose; it will most likely attract the same experiences. These experiences will, then, reaffirm the rightness you have about these situations.

If it is possible to go straight to content reframing, then you will no longer form such beliefs in the first place. Sadly, many people tend to dwell on the negative experience. This causes them to have similar negative experiences. The worse thing is that they do not realize the connection, and they become surprised when they continue to experience negativity in their lives.

It is important to realize that situations are neither bad nor good. It is only the way you view them that makes them bad or good. If you choose to view them as a negative thing, then you will form a negative or limiting belief that causes you to have the same experiences that affirm such a negative belief. If you continue to do this, your negative beliefs will deepen and worsen over time.

If you focus on the negative, you filter out your experiences, causing you to repeat your negative beliefs. For example, you have just gotten out of an abusive relationship. Your former partner cheated and treated you badly. Obviously, this experience has had a huge effect on you.

Then again, would you learn from it and do your best to avoid making the same mistakes or would you start to believe that all men are liars, cheaters, and bad people? If you choose the latter, then you have already formed a limiting belief, which is not healthy for you.

To change limiting beliefs, you should acquire more data about situations. Do not disregard the positive facts by solely focusing on the negative. When you see negative aspects, view them in a rational manner and find out if they are indeed facts that are truthful.

Another way to eliminate your negative beliefs is to spend a few minutes every day affirming a totally different belief.

Five minutes for every new belief is enough if you have a busy day.

You should do this in a quiet place without distractions. Focus on your affirmation and refrain from having any other thoughts. Control your mind so that you do not imagine anything unnecessary. Concentrate on the words so you can fully grasp what they mean.

This exercise is effective because it lets you hypnotize yourself lightly. You only focus on one thing. The induced hypnosis causes you to directly move all your beliefs into your subconscious mind.

Some people think that it is their conscious mind that manifests thoughts into reality. What they do not know is that it is their subconscious mind that makes this happen. Ideally, you should practice this technique every day for thirty days. Each day, you will notice a slight change until eventually, you will reflect your new beliefs.

# Chapter 8:
# Choosing to Live Without Negativity

Presently after that segment of settling on the correct choice, I trust that we would all be able to concur that a standout amongst the most moral decisions to make in our lives is to dispose of negative considerations and emotions.

Negative reasoning can have a significantly ruinous effect on all parts of our lives. It is never great. When you are drawn into this example of negative reasoning, you are building a jail in your own special personality, holding you as the detainee.

Many individuals attempt separated approaches to break out of their negative idea designs, just to whip themselves and aggravate it. On the off chance that you are battling with negative reasoning, it is conceivable to turn things around and develop internal peace and satisfaction.

In any case, initially, you should submit! You should submit yourself and work hard to expel negative musings and to make an extraordinary level of satisfaction that will remain on until what's to come.

Here are the four keys to break free of pessimism for good:

## Perceive your negative thinking patterns

Negative idea designs are tedious, useless considerations. They don't have any genuine reason, but to influence you to have negative feelings, for example, outrage or gloom.

When you figure out how to perceive and distinguish these negative idea designs as they happen, you can begin to define a choice with respect to how to respond.

## Move away from negative thinkers

Individuals who are influenced by negative musings feel miserable on the grounds that they don't realize what to do. It might appear as though there are insufficient responses to confront your issues, to enable you to get ready for the future and manage distinctive circumstances.

So how would you travel through the course of days in a way that is astute and honest to goodness without getting inundated in these critical contemplations? All things considered, you should watch your contemplations! To wind up noticeably free of antagonism, you should be made more mindful of your contemplations and what you put into your cerebrum. Begin to spend more regard for what is happening inside your psyche at any gave time.

Particularly, put all your consideration far from negative reasoning that might emerge. In the event that you see something that incenses or stresses you, do your best to fathom it before it turns into an issue! Turn into a mindful spectator of what goes ahead in your internal condition.

Each time your inward mindfulness is conveyed to a negative idea design, it is just assaulting you and convincing you to build up your brain in that capacity. Simply ahead and check whether you can locate these negative musings when they emerge before they pick up excessively compel. In the event that you can't locate these opposite thoughts at to start with, at that point you do have another opportunity to wind up noticeably more mindful of them and to react with positive musings. For instance, when a negative feeling becomes an integral factor, you can redirect your regard for the suppositions of energy that are being produced by such thoughts.

## Wind up noticeably mindful

When you have negative considerations, they hover under two headings. The main turn the past; they help you to remember your slips, obstructions, blame, and anything in your life that did not go the way you wished it did. The second is the consistent stress without bounds, and it makes you dreadful of what might possibly happen to yourself or others.

We will find out about this later in this book, however, these steady stresses can appear as worry about whether you will accomplish singular objectives or uneasiness about the security of your funds or connections. Or on the other hand, possibly you stress over seeming old. To get past these critical idea designs, your mind needs to cast its attention on the past or future.

To end up plainly more completely alert and ready to advance out of this reasoning example of stress, stress, and dread; you should divert your consideration and contemplations into the without further ado. Give your present minute your whole full focus.

## Pick constructive thoughts over destructive thoughts

In this way, now that you built up some inward mindfulness you can intentionally choose to change your reasoning with the goal that it is useful as opposed to ruinous. Being sure is a decision. Being negative is additionally a decision.

When you enable yourself to think productively, you enable yourself to be glad when things are either going right or when things are turning out badly. When you accept usefully, you place issues into the point of view and for all intents and purposes manage them.

Expelling yourself from antagonism won't occur immediately. You should practice and practice to show signs of improvement at it. The more you build up this mindfulness in your idea designs, the more you can utilize your brain to develop joy. To evacuate mental mess, you just need to step up with regards to expel them and to confer yourself further.

# Chapter 9:
# Why Declutter Your Mind

One of the most prominent reasons you want to declutter your mind is because it already is playing a negative role in your life. You may be experiencing its effect right now and may want to do something about it.

Most of the available resources we find online and in print when we look for help point out to dealing with the effects of a cluttered mind. This is just like traditional medicine nowadays which uses treatment to deal with the symptoms and not with what is causing the symptoms.

All these pieces of advice have a valid point. But in the end, if you look carefully at the bigger picture, you have to admit that something is missing. No matter how hard you try and succeed in tackling the symptoms that derive from a cluttered mind, you will need to address the central issue you are facing eventually. Your account is slowly and steadily becoming your enemy – the cluttering creeps in, step by step, and only by realizing and reversing this process will you be able to put an end to this spiral of unhappiness.

The benefits derived from dealing with the cause rather than the effects are enormous.

# Being Efficient

It is hard not to notice that many of us who try to engage in dealing with problems we're facing in our day-to-day life have limited amounts of energy to spend. We all have to be productive, stay healthy, take care of others that rely on us for their well-being; and at the same time, we have a job or are searching for a job, we are part of a family or a relationship, we have our dreams, desires, needs.

The obvious question arises: is it worth fighting to deal with our problems in such a way that we spend a great deal of time and resources? Does this struggle end eventually? Are we efficient? I'm afraid the honest answer is not a positive one.

# Vicious Circle

As I mentioned before, most of the resources that are available for those who strive to achieve happiness in their lives are limited to dealing with the symptoms and not the cause. Moreover, we can observe a pattern that develops. How so?

When we approach an issue that is causing distress by tackling the problem in itself, not only do we lose perspective, but we enter a merry-go-round that takes up a lot of effort and energy and gives us the illusion that we are advancing towards our goal. After we deal with social anxiety by making new friends, the next issue presents itself, for we've spent a lot of money and time and now we felt insecure and stressed over our cost on day-to-day living. If we work more to cover those new expenses, we

53

end up stressed, tired, unable to maintain the relationships we just developed, and hence we get a new form of social anxiety. And even worse, we feel disappointed, and we blame ourselves for that.

## Stop. Take a Step Back. Unclutter Your Mind.

We just don't know it could be done with little effort. We have no idea that we stand close to the solution, for we are not examining the correct obstacles. The following chapters will put things in perspective and deal with more detailed aspects of the core concept. For now, keep in mind that there is hardly anyone that can do this on his or her own. Knowledge is power, but at the same time, learning is shared and accumulated not as limited individuals, but as a collective mind that continually improves.

For now, you already feel the answer to the "Why declutter your mind?" question. So let's engage in building up the whole perspective.

When you clear out mental clutter and its symptoms, it can make you feel as if you are **peeling onions**.

Imagine yourself trying to peel off all the layers of the onion so that you can get to the core. This is what decluttering does to your mind. It peels back all your thoughts and ideas. You peel away that which your cluttered thoughts made you believe to get down to your truth.

Everyone has experienced moments of profound love, peace, connection, and clarity once all the layers are peeled away. These moments occur when the mind is already clutter-free.

Anyway, before you learn about the exercises that eliminate negative thinking, you should understand the reason why you have such thoughts. The following are the most common causes of mental clutter: Daily Stress

Too much stress is the main reason why so many people feel overwhelmed. In fact, stress caused by information overload, endless options, and physical clutter can trigger various mental health issues, including depression, anxiety, and panic attacks.

# Chapter 10:
# How Minds Get Cluttered?

So how do our brains get cluttered? Well, everyone has either clutter accumulated in their minds. In this chapter, we will go over some of the reasons responsible for your brain getting cluttered with negative thoughts. We will tackle ways to prevent cluttering, and we will have a look into one of the most common ways to break the clutter – living a simpler life.

As we already settled, the best way to declutter your mind is to be informed on why your brain is cluttered in the first place. In other words, one of the main reasons people have so much negative energy is because they lack knowledge regarding brain clutter. The majority of the population does not know what confusion is and explains it as something entirely different, blaming either the context, others, or themselves.

The mechanism that clutters our mind is fueled by our uncertainty and social conventions. We live in a society that praises individualism, success, strength, and determination.

When we face obstacles in achieving those, clutter begins to form. But is there a way to prevent it from happening in the first place?

There is good news and bad news. The good news is, being self-aware and having a more relaxed view of things can positively prevent the start of the clustering process. The bad news is, staying confident and comfortable, without stress about small and insignificant things is virtually impossible nowadays.

As we stated before, there are many similarities between the cluttering and a common disease that affects our body. As is the case with the prevalent condition, to prevent, we have to take care of our bodies, to avoid exposing ourselves to evil influences. It's safe to say that the mind follows the same pattern. To prevent clutter, we should not prove ourselves to bad habits, - stress, strong stimuli, overload of info -. Sounds pretty good, but it is tough.

There is no way we could pass through life without interacting with what the present times hold. Unless we choose from the start to isolate ourselves from all that is human and social, becoming monks or taking the ascetic road, it is evident that we have to deal with the challenges and not run away from it.

Going even further with the comparison, a body that wants to prevent illness and disease cannot merely run away from pathogens, isolate from any possible harm. That would achieve the opposite results: our immune system would not be formed, we would become weak and more exposed to getting sick. The same can be applied to our mind. It is never a solution to stay away, and even if some precautions should be taken, living life to the full is the way to go about it. What if all of us choose to get away, to run from each other and isolate ourselves. Hard to imagine, isn't it?

We all know that when falling in love, for example, there is a great deal of risk that love will eventually cause suffering.

But that never stopped anyone from searching for love. We know the price, and we are happily ready to pay it. It is part of our existence, so we don't even question it.

The same applies to our mind and the risk of cluttering. Preventing the formation of such clutter is a definite possibility, but acting upon what our immense, complex, and beautiful soul reveals is not debatable. We cannot just put half of our brain on pause. It wouldn't be fair; it wouldn't benefit anyone. So, we can only rely on staying on top of things, being informed and accessing the knowledge that could prevent the creeping in of clutter while at the same time enjoy the vast array of possibilities that derive from it.

## Simplifying Your Life to achieve happiness

One of the funniest things related to the act of simplifying our lives is that this is a genuinely complex and complicated endeavor. Paradoxical, right? How can streamline something can be confused? Well, anyone that ever tried this knows exactly how hard and not at all simple it can be.

The new millennium brought into our lives a sense of time that is quickly running away from us, an infinite amount of knowledge that bombards us form some different sources.

Even though it is hard to say these scientific and social achievements are harmful, for it wouldn't be fair, it is entirely appropriate to take a step back and think again. Are those developments that we benefit from today directly connected to our level of happiness? Or, on the contrary, they tend to get in the way of us achieving serenity, joyfulness, and bliss.

Simplifying our lives doesn't mean making it miserable, or cutting ourselves from the delights of the modern society. Instead, it could suggest getting to make a careful selection and filtering of what enriches us. Once we get hold of that, by being honest with ourselves, we could start focusing on that and leaving all the detrimental side-activities outside of our horizon. Unfortunately, this is way easier said than done.

# Chapter 11:
# Types of Mental Clutter

Mental clutter takes up plenty of space in your brain, making it harder to think through decisions and to enjoy life. If we let it, psychological confusion will move and permanently soak inside our minds, developing a pattern that results in a full absorption of our spiritual energy and health. Our firm belief is that with just a little work, we can all find a way to cleanse our minds and move forward. But first, we must explore the types of mental clutter that exists, so that we become aware and can spot them when they arise. The faster we detect some symptoms, the better:

These are the types of mental clutter that can be incredibly damaging over the long-term:

## Worry

Worrying is never good. In fact, it's entirely unproductive. And on some levels, we believe that through worrying we can prevent specific events from unfolding and that we can control our future. However, it's up to us to act in such situations as they arise. The ability of our minds to project itself to the future is a fantastic skill. Just like the possibility to recall the past and learn from it. However, there is a catch: when imagining the future, we do so not by engaging in a rational analysis of facts and info, but we mix emotions, feelings, fear, and uncertainty. Hence, whatever the future holds for us becomes an obstacle in our present moment.

Worry is the most popular form of clutter as it blocks your mind from all sorts of gunk and leaves your brainless room for creativity or problem-solving. As powerful a brain can be, it positively cannot deal with the vast array of difficulties and issues that come up in our ordinary day-to-day road through life. It isn't fair to ask such things of ourselves or our mind.

On the other hand, as high as it may seem at first glance, not worrying enough can also become a problem and make room for clutter. Most of us feel that worrying is detrimental and thus they take refuge in all sorts of escaping methods, either by overlooking the obstacles or by running away from issues and problems into destructive habits, dependencies, abuse of substances or chaotic behavior. We will talk extensively about these problems in a further chapter.

## Regret

One of the most visible forms of clutter is through repentance. Now, you must know that there is not a single successful or happy person who has never decided that they've regretted one or more actions or events from their past. We all mourn something, and we all make mistakes. It's part of what makes us human. However, it's up to us to decide whether we will let our mistakes define us or we will learn from them and move forward towards our well-being.

And by the way, we don't have to repeat our mistakes. We all heard that many times. Don't repeat your mistakes, don't engage in actions that follow a destructive pattern, and find the power to change when you've made a mistake. It is still tough to do. It would mean we can both live our lives and also observe ourselves objectively and identify soft spots to work on. Even though it is hard or seems impossible most of the times, it is a substantial possibility, once we get hold of our mind and its tricks. If we acknowledge this fact, we can begin to see the past decisions or recollections that inspire us to feel regret as an opportunity to learn and change ourselves in positive ways. Disappointment is always unhelpful if it does not bring about learning or personal change. We could call it a waste. We can never change the past, but we can always change the future. We can make positive choices today, to prevent future regrettable decisions.

You know how they say there's something good about every evil thing. This is the case of regret; if we keep an open mind, regretting will teach us to finally accept past mistakes as an inevitable part of life and practice the critical art of forgiveness.

## Guilt

Life is always about moving forward., But sin keeps us in the past, usually because we ponder about what we should or should not have done in certain situations. As you can imagine, our mind has the infinite ability to develop scenarios. It is a never-ending story. We all have been there. What if I would have said that, maybe I could have changed the outcome. The feeling of guilt is a strong motivator that keeps our mind focused on the past. Always reevaluating, always trying to absolve ourselves of any mistakes we've made. These mechanisms that our brain develop to keep us safe and comfortable can sooner or later have a big price. If not addressed wisely, after a while, guilt can soak into your brain, and it'll be almost impossible to move forward. It is not realistic to say that you'll forget what happened, but it is possible to release the past to live in the present.

**Negative Self-talk**

Our beliefs regarding ourselves, others, and the world as a whole can profoundly impact what we often say about others, our circumstances, and ourselves. Piece by piece and step by step, what we believe influences what we say and what we say defines how we behave. These belief systems we build for ourselves originate from many experiences we accumulate over our lifetime. One does not merely become a negative self-talker in a day; it takes years for such a mentality to take place, but the reality is not very encouraging. So many of us misinterpret life circumstances, failures, other people's behavior and we tend to take them upon themselves.

But as we all know, negative self-talk is one of the worse mental clutters that can lower our self-esteem and hurt others even if it happens indirectly. When you boldly declare something as being insulting or not very complimenting about yourself, it creeps into your belief system and slowly but surely will manifest later in your life.

Attitude makes the difference! You might recall the famous words of one the most impressive politician of the UK, Winston Churchill, who said: "Attitude is a small thing that makes a big difference." We couldn't agree more. If you go through life thinking that you are not good enough, you will never be good enough. It's that simple. Go through your life being self-aware, but try to figure out all the changes that you need to make. Not what others tell you, but what you feel about that. Write them all down. What are the life changes that you must make, as you think it in your core, in your bones? That's the moment when you establish the foundational point to get you started.

# Chapter 12: Maintaining a decluttered mind

While your body reacts to worry through your sensory system, a few stressors may emerge at certain anticipated circumstances—on your drive to work, when on a gathering with your manager, or even family social events, for instance. Presently to deal with such unsurprising stressors, you either change the current circumstance or change how you respond to it. Whichever alternative you choose to follow up on, dependably think about these four A's: keep away from, adjust, adjust, or acknowledge.

## Stay away from unnecessary stress

It may appear to be unfortunate to maintain a strategic distance from a distressing circumstance that should be tended to, however shockingly, there are a few stressors throughout your life that you can wipe out by unadulterated evasion.

Figure out how to state "no" – Know your impediments and stick to them. Regardless of whether it is your expert or individual life, a surefire formula for being worried is the point at which you take more than you can deal with. Separate your "should" and "must" and, when conceivable, say "no" to going up against excessively and remain on it.

Keep away from or avoid individuals who worry you – If somebody is a reliable reason for worry in your life, at that point constrain the measure of time you go through with that individual, or better still end the association with such individual.

Take control of your condition – If the prospect of the nightly news makes you restless, kill the TV. On the off chance that been in rush hour gridlock influences you to tense, take a more drawn out however less-voyaged course. On the off chance that heading off to the market is something you hate and find as a repulsive errand, simply do your shopping for food on the web.

## Modify the situation

On the off chance that you have taken a stab at dodging as much as you can an unpleasant circumstance, at that point have a go at circumventing it. Frequently, this may include changing the way you convey and work each day.

Rather than smothering/packaging your sentiments, express it. On the off chance that something or somebody you know is disturbing you, be more decisive and direct to the individual and convey your worries transparently and consciously. On the off chance that you have an exam/meeting to contemplate for and your loquacious flatmate/companion just returned home or came around, say in advance that you just have five minutes to talk. In the event that you don't voice your sentiments, hatred will manufacture, and the pressure will increment since you need to get together with examining.

Compromise on your characters. When you request that somebody changes their conduct, be set up to do likewise if require be. In the event that you both will twist no less than a bit, you'll have a decent shot of finding a glad center ground to play on.

Deal with your chance better. Poor time administration we definitely know can cause a great deal of pressure. Be that as it may, in the event that you design and ensuring you don't overextend yourself past your points of confinement, you'll see it less demanding to remain quiet and concentrated on your objectives.

Be more decisive and direct. Try not to assume a lower priority in your own life. Manage each of your issues head-on, and doing your best to expect and in addition anticipate them. Like I referred to prior, in the event that you have an exam to think about for and your glib flatmate just returned home, say in advance that you just have five minutes to talk.

## Adjust to the stressor

How your musings are can profoundly affect your feelings of anxiety. Each time you contemplate yourself and the conditions around you, you draw in greater pessimism to yourself, making your body respond as though it were in the throes of a strain filled circumstance. Recapture your feeling of control by changing your desires and your state of mind to unpleasant circumstances.

Reframe issues. Attempt to see distressing circumstances from a more positive point of view. As opposed to raging about a road turned parking lot, take a gander at it as a chance to stop and regroup, tune in to your most loved radio station, or appreciate some alone time.

Take a gander at the 10,000-foot view. Take a full point of view of the upsetting circumstance. Ask yourself how vital it will be over the long haul. Will it matter in a month? A year? Is it worth getting furious about? In the event that the appropriate response is no, center your opportunity and vitality somewhere else.

Ask yourself how key changing it will be over the long haul. Modify your guidelines. Compulsiveness is an essential source through which one can be worried up. Quit setting yourself up for disappointment by requesting flawlessness regardless of your demeanor. Set sensible and achievable norms for yourself as well as other people, and figure out how to approve of "sufficient."

## Acknowledge the things you can't change

Go on. Try not to be hesitant to acknowledge the things you can't change which don't appear to be variable.

A few wellsprings of stress are unavoidable. You can't avoid or change stressors, for example, the passing of a friend or family member, the event of a serious disease, or even a national retreat. In these cases, the most ideal approach to adapt to pressure is simply to acknowledge things as they seem to be. Acknowledgment might be troublesome, yet over the long haul, it's simpler than railing against a circumstance you can't change.

Try not to endeavor to control the wild. You are not a Supreme Being. Numerous things that occur in life are route outside our ability to control—especially the conduct and state of mind other individuals depict. Instead of worrying about them and attempting to transform it, concentrate on the things you have control over them, for example, the way you respond to these issues.

Search for the upside in these circumstances. When confronting huge difficulties dissect and take a gander at them as chances to put resources into your self-improvement. In the event that your own poor decisions offered ascend to an upsetting circumstance, contemplate on them and gain from your missteps.

Figure out how to excuse. Acknowledge the way that we live in a blemished world and that individuals are inclined to committing an error. Relinquish all the outrage and feelings of disdain and simply free yourself from negative vitality by pardoning them and proceeding onward with your life.

Practice the specialty of demonstrating appreciation. At the point when the stretch is getting you down and is turning you back to front, pause for a minute to think about every one of the things you acknowledge in your life, including your positive qualities and blessings. This straightforward methodology can enable you to keep things in context and influence you to see that you are still on track with your life objectives.

# Chapter 13:
# Decluttering your thoughts

Before we plunge into the different activities to take out your negative reasoning, it's fundamental initially to comprehend why you have these contemplations. Along these lines, in this area, we'll go more than four reasons for the mental mess.

## Daily Stress

An exorbitant amount of stress is the essential reason many individuals feel overpowered by life. Indeed, the weight made by data over-burden, physical mess, and the unlimited decisions required from these things can trigger a variety of emotional wellness issues like summed up nervousness, freeze assaults, and gloom.

Couple this worry with the authentic stresses and worries throughout your life, and you may wind up with rest issues, muscle torment, migraines, chest torment, visit diseases, and stomach and intestinal issue.

## The Paradox of Choice

The flexibility of decision, something venerated in free social orders, can have a reducing purpose of return with regards to psychological well-being. Therapist Barry Schwartz authored the adage "mystery of decision," which entireties up his discoveries that expanded decision prompts more tension, hesitation, loss of motion, and disappointment. More alternatives may manage the cost of unbiasedly better outcomes; however, they won't make you upbeat.

## Too Much "Stuff."

Our homes are loaded with garments we never wear, books we won't read, toys that are unused, and devices that don't see the light of day. Our PC inboxes are flooding. Our work areas are jumbled, and our telephones are blazing messages like "You require more stockpiling."

With this consistent stream of data and access to innovation, getting to be plainly mass purchasers of things and information is less demanding than any time in recent memory. At the snap of a catch, we can arrange anything from a book to a speedboat and have it conveyed to our doorstep.

We're filling our homes with things we don't need and filling our chance with a constant flow of tweets, refreshes, articles, blog entries, and feline recordings. Data and stuff are heaping up around us, but then we feel vulnerable to make a move.

The greater part of this unessential stuff and information suck our chance and efficiency, as well as produces responsive, on edge, and negative contemplations.

We regularly feel like we don't have room schedule-wise to clean up in light of the fact that we're excessively bustling devouring new stuff and data. In any case, sooner or later, this hastiness is driving us to mental and enthusiastic depletion. As we process everything coming at us, we investigate, ruminate, and stress ourselves to the limit.

How have we dismissed the qualities and life needs that once kept us adjusted and rational? What would we be able to do about it? We can't backpedal in time and live without innovation. We can't disavow the greater part of our common belonging and abide in a surrender. We need to make sense of an approach to live in this cutting-edge world without losing our rational soundness.

Cleaning up our stuff and curtailing time went through with our advanced gadgets helps dispose of a portion of the tension and negative reasoning. Yet, despite everything we have a lot of motivation to lose all sense of direction in the psychological mess of a negative idea, stress, and lament.

We stress over our wellbeing, our occupations, our children, the economy, our connections, what we look like, what other individuals consider us, psychological warfare, governmental issues, torment from the past, and our unusual prospects. Our musings about these things influence us to endure and undermine the joy we could encounter at this moment on the off chance that we didn't have that consistent voice in our heads mixing things up.

## The Negativity Bias

The human sensory system has been advancing for 600 million years, yet despite everything, it reacts the same as our initial human progenitors who confronted hazardous circumstances all the time and required simply to survive.

# Meditation

You don't need to be a Buddhist, a spiritualist, or a precious stone conveying ex-radical to rehearse contemplation. You can have a place with any profound or religious confidence or have no religious association at all to receive the rewards of reflection and utilize it as an instrument for cleaning up your psyche.

In the event that you've never drilled contemplation, or you're not acquainted with it, you may be put off by sitting discreetly in the lotus position and purging your psyche. In any case, don't let the banalities about pondering cavern inhabitants keep you from trying its attempt.

Reflection has been polished for a huge number of years and begins in antiquated Buddhist, Hindu, and Chinese customs. There are many styles of thoughtful practices, however, most strategies start with similar advances—sitting unobtrusively, concentrating consideration on your breath, and expelling any diversions that come in your direction.

The objective of contemplation changes relying upon the kind of reflection hone and the coveted result of the meditator. For our motivations here, we propose contemplation as an instrument to enable you to prepare your brain and control your musings, both when you are sitting in reflection and when you aren't.

The advantages of reflecting convert into your everyday life, helping you control stress and overthinking, and giving a large group of medical advantages that we'll examine underneath.

The way to discovering fulfillment with contemplation only is to hone. By making a day by day responsibility regarding reflection, you will enhance your abilities and find how the psychological, physical, and enthusiastic advantages increment after some time.

Here is a basic 11-step process you can use to manufacture the contemplation propensity:

Select a tranquil, quiet space for your contemplation hone where you can close the way to be totally alone.

Decide a particular time of day for your training. In the event that you've started a profound breathing practice, you can utilize this as your trigger (and beginning stage) for your new contemplation propensity. Or on the other hand, you can pick another trigger and work on ruminating at some other time of day.

Choose whether you need to reflect sitting on a cushion on the floor or in a straight-back seat or couch. Make an effort not to lean back as you think about, since you may nod off.

Evacuate all diversions and kill every single advanced gadget or different gadgets that make a commotion. Expel pets from the room.

# Set a clock for 10 minutes.

Sit easily either in a seat or leg over the leg on the floor with a pad. Keep your spine erect and your hands resting delicately in your lap.

Close your eyes, or keep them open with a descending centered look, at that point take a couple of profound purifying breaths through your nose—we suggest three or four breaths at any given moment.

Bit by bit wind up noticeably mindful of your relaxing. Notice the air moving in and out through your nostrils and the ascent and fall of your chest and stomach area. Enable your breaths to fall into place easily, without compelling them.

Concentrate on the impression of breathing, maybe even rationally thinking "in" as you breathe in and "out" as you breathe out.

Your musings will meander a great deal first and foremost. Each time they do, tenderly let them go and after that arrival your thoughtfulness regarding the impression of relaxing.

Try not to judge yourself for having nosy contemplations. That is only your "monkey mind" attempting to assume control. Just lead your brain back to concentrated consideration on relaxing. You may need to do this dozens of times at first.

As you concentrate on breathing, you'll likely notice different recognitions and sensations like sounds, physical

75

inconvenience, feelings, and so forth. Simply advise these as they emerge in your mindfulness, and afterward tenderly come back to the energy of relaxing.

You will likely progressively turn into the observer to all sounds, sensations, feelings, and contemplations as they emerge and pass away. View them just as you are watching them from a separation without judgment or private remark.

As opposed to your mind taking control and fleeing at whatever point an idea or diversion happens, you, in the long run, acquire and more energy of your record and your capacity to divert it back to the present.

At the outset, you'll feel you're in a steady fight with your monkey mind. In any case, with training, you won't have to divert your considerations dependably. Considerations start to drop away normally, and your record opens up to the tremendous stillness and immensity of simply being available. This is a really tranquil, fulfilling knowledge.

Contemplation experts allude to this space of stillness as the "hole"— the noiseless space between musings. At in the first place, the hole is extremely tight, and it's hard to stay there for more than a couple of nanoseconds. As you turn into a more honed meditator, you'll discover the hole opens more extensive and all the more as often as possible, and you can rest in it for more expanded timeframes.

You can encounter a concise snapshot of the space between contemplations by attempting this activity: Close your eyes and start to see your considerations. Just watch them travel every which way for a couple of moments. At that point make the inquiry, "Where will my next idea originate from?" Stop and sit tight for the appropriate response. You may see there's a short hole in your reasoning while you anticipate the answer.

# Chapter 14:
# Importance of Decluttering Distractions that Cause Stress and Anxiety

When you take yourself off the grid, you remove the distractions that you encounter on a daily basis. These are the ones that cause your stress, fears, frustrations, and anger. When you wrestle with life, whether in your work, family, school, or religion, you should get rid of all the external influences that contribute to your worries and anxiety.

## Eliminating the Distraction

Many people have the desire to reduce distractions, but they are not able to do it because they are full of excuses. Their reasoning may not even be justified. If you are one of these people, your purpose may not have your best intentions in mind and at heart.

"If I lose my mobile phone service, an emergency may happen, and I won't be able to get in touch with anybody."

"What if somebody needed to get a hold of me?"

"If I receive an e-mail on the weekend, I have to answer it. Otherwise, my boss will think that I am not working."

"I feel bored when there is nothing for me to do."

"I enjoy having a busy week and having lots of tasks to accomplish."

"I might miss out on certain things."

It can be challenging to get rid of distractions at first. You will always find a way to make an excuse. However, once you get over the initial heartbreak of disconnecting, you will realize that the circumstances are not that bad.

Why Is It Important to Declutter the Distractions that Cause You to Be Anxious?

*Getting Rid of Distractions Helps You Slow Down.* Your body is not the only thing that moves a lot; your mind does too. You exhaust your mind thinking about your daily chores and tasks. The distractions around you make matters worse by draining your account further. What you can do to rejuvenate your mind is rejuvenated your body. You need to take a break from **all** the action to avoid **breaking down**.

*Getting Rid of Distractions Help You Focus on One Thing at a Time.* When there isn't anything that distracts you, it becomes easier to concentrate on what is right in front of you. This could be anything, from spending time with your family and friends to writing a book to complete a project. When there is no distraction, you can devote all your intentions and efforts to one thing at a time.

*Getting Rid of Distractions Allows You to Put Everything into Perspective.* Not everything is a big deal. Recognize the fact that there are times when you tend to make significant issues out of small problems. You add

unnecessary stress to your day, which is why you feel even
more anxious. When you get rid of distractions, you can see
life for what it is rather than what you make it out to be.

# Chapter 15:
# Investing in Yourself

## What is investing in yourself?

What strikes a chord when you hear the word contributing? Does it mean, putting your cash in protection, common supports, money markets or even high return speculations? Other individuals may just consider spending when they are going to bite the dust, and they haven't left anything for their posterity.

Many individuals even put vigorously in wellbeing supplements, fitness coaches and beauticians to influence themselves to live more, more advantageous or additionally look more youthful! Envision the promoting spending plan for magnificence organizations these days.

The most fundamental and No.1 run is to "Put resources into Yourself. In the event that you don't, who else will?

Your folks will just put resources into your instruction until the point when you leave school. Yet, that is only the necessities and does not show you significant lessons about money related proficiency.

Would you rely upon schools or colleges to show you how to profit? Most schools just show you aptitudes, so you can gain cash working for other individuals. What about business college? Truly, if business speakers are such specialists in business, why are despite everything they addressing there as opposed to making a fortune in business wanders?

Would your supervisor show you how to prevail in business with the goal that one day, you will be in his position?

You and just you must be sufficiently proactive to assume that liability.

When you put resources into yourself, it implies going up against the significance of instructing yourself. Try not to trust that training is restricted to the scholarly or specialized sense, however, they are important abilities to be produced throughout everyday life. Our insight does not and ought not to stop at school.

For most working grown-ups, their training enters an impediment arrange after they leave school. They quit learning, and in this manner, they quit developing.

We realize that IQ is critical right? In any case, for what reason aren't the keenest individuals on the planet the wealthiest individuals on the planet? There are numerous bookkeepers and money related organizers hurrying to their autos each night endeavoring to beat the after-work movement! They are not rich!

So how is putting resources into yourself done?

Wander off in fantasy land a bit.

What have you generally needed to attempt? Present's an ideal opportunity to plan exactly that — whatever it is. Skydive, get up a half hour early consistently to compose that Great American Novel, visit a nearby fascination that you've generally been interested about however never made an appearance at — whatever.

Setting aside the opportunity to accomplish something that you've for a long while been itching to do is a method for demonstrating to yourself that YOU are essential. You'll feel fierier and simply better all in all. Like that old business says, "you're justified, despite all the trouble!".

## Take in another ability.

Truly, this could include taking a class or taking in another aptitude. Be that as it may, it could likewise mean perusing up regarding a matter utilizing books from the library, or downloading a French podcast and rehearsing each day. Or on the other hand, it could mean joining a weaving club for fledglings and adapting together in a gathering. Hell, it could even propose currently attempting to enhance your score in the most recent cell phone amusement.

The fact of the matter is to explore new territory that requires practice and exertion. Practicing your mind helps keep it sharp, and makes life a mess all the more intriguing.

## Get over an old hindrance.

We as a whole have things that are keeping us down, shielding us from being the general population we truly could be in the event that we worked through an issue. Possibly you stress constantly or are unbelievably timid yet long to have companions. Or then again maybe your financial records is overdrawn constantly and you and your mate are continually battling for cash.

It's the ideal opportunity for a change. Get directing, get treatment, get whatever it takes to get over that old hindrance and move past it. It's one venture that will be WELL justified, despite all the trouble.

## Make sound propensities.

Eat well, get enough rest, and exercise every day. Sound propensities give you the vitality to DO the things you need to do, instead of keeping running down and debilitated. There's in no way like dealing with yourself to enhance the nature of your life.

## Offer yourself a reprieve.

At long last, a standout amongst the most disregarded approaches to putting resources into yourself is simply to offer yourself a reprieve every once in a while. In case you're so finished booked that you're generally worried from hurrying all over, drop something. You don't have to do everything. We as a whole need breaks, and you are no special case. Back rubs are extraordinary, however just doing nothing is a phenomenal break as well. At the point when was the last time, you booked a do-nothing day?

The exact opposite thing staying after you start perusing, tuning in and partner is to execute all that you have learned. Try not to give these assignments a chance to threaten you and begin applying with extra special care.

Similarly, as Rome wasn't worked in a day, it will set aside the opportunity to aggregate information and follow up on it. Be that as it may, it is a basic advance in light of the fact that no experience will consistently bring any outcome unless it is followed up on. To know and not to do isn't to know!

Thus, begin now and put resources into yourself, build up the fundamental aptitudes for progress, and acquire the most noteworthy return you will ever get. Here's to your prosperity!

## Instructions to Achieve What You Want in Life

On the off chance that you have a fantasy, a conspicuous and daring objective that you need to accomplish, you will require an arrangement of fitting abilities. You can discover a huge number of tips regarding this matter, yet no place else will you see a basic rundown of 2-3 most vital abilities which when organized, will ensure your coveted outcome. Why would that be? Since not very many think about it and those that do – well they need to keep it a mystery or offer it with few.

I have been ordering this learning a little bit at a time all through as long as I can remember, continually applying these basic yet hugely powerful standards and I might want to leave this experience for descendants and each one of the individuals who will tune in. It is the most satisfying and exceptional feeling one can accomplish, to have the capacity to take an interest in the prosperity of his

85

colleagues. I don't have anything to stow away on the grounds that exclusive a couple of you will have the capacity to tune in and apply these standards, lamentably. Then again, the way that you try to secure information places you in a flawless place. As hard as it is to accept, there are not all that many like you.

Keep in mind that your arrangement of convictions or what you have confidence in is your most fantastic guide throughout everyday life. All that you think turns into your existence, so it is crucial to think inaccurate standards, in something that is for sure evident. The greater part of individuals today think in made up things without acknowledging it. They battle devils and ghosts. In this manner, they can never control their lives. Search for reality, and you will discover it! Try not to enable anybody to mentally program you, and by somebody, I mean merchants, government officials, religious enthusiasts thus called "researchers." Today it has turned out to be so normal to confide in science, allude to logical research albeit present-day researchers have made more "evil spirits" than any alchemists or voodoo men. Get your declaration of everything that you're learning and manufacture your arrangement of convictions in light of such establishments.

## Be consistent with your wants

SECOND, no less of a vital expertise is to know precisely what you need out of life. Figure out what you need in the first place, second, et cetera. What cost would you say you will pay? You either pay in advance, for instance by venturing out of your customary range of familiarity, with your opportunity and diligent work, or you pay later, for example by losing your flexibility, companions, family, wellbeing or with adding up to frustration throughout everyday life. Continuously think about the results! On the off chance that you don't recognize what you need out of life, it will be loaded with episodes, and not extremely lovely ones at that. In this way, design your life or else somebody will set it up for you! The best technique for arranging is to record it on paper. Dreams, preponderances, supplications, reflections, representations – THESE are imperative. Be that as it may, anything not composed down.

The ability to think big, creatively and at the same time to be able to focus on a goal is not an easy task. Therefore, learning is required. For starters, you would need to master specific thinking tools – concentration, visualization and mind-mapping is the necessary minimum. Planning on paper and not just in your head using a mind map allows you to learn and to think efficiently, intelligently, and so fast that no other genius of the past can ever compare.

## Never stop. Affirm and visualize.

FOURTH, an essential skill for achieving goals is to learn about strengths in yourself and discard any and all excuses and persevere to the end! By using the third power described above (the cycle of achievement) and observing how one comes up with all kinds of excuses not to do anything, learn to discard such explanations and persevere to the end. Affirmations and visualizations can help here.

Of course, this isn't a complete list of skills but is sufficient to achieve practically any realistic goal. The ability to communicate effectively can also be added to this list although for some it is one of the innate qualities or is developed within the family. If you were not gifted in this area, self-education and knowledge of the essential laws of communication could help you.

## The Golden Rule

One of those laws is so called the Golden Rule: "Do unto others as you would have them do unto you." You just need to remember that it is not only a mere wish or a good rule of behavior in society, but it is one of the harshest laws of the universe. Because people will always treat you the way, you treat them. Lying, deceit, hypocrisy, violence, stealing, poverty and sickness in your life are the result of your dishonesty, disrespect, fraud, greed, and hatred for others. In the same respect, joy, health, abundance, success, and happiness is the result of your love and selfless service to others. This type of service is the key to prosperity, personal growth, and happiness. Make it your habit. Serve everyone you meet – at home, at work, at play.

Service, however, doesn't mean doing their job instead of them. Make service part of your mental attitude. Whatever you do, don't do it because you must, not out of obligation, not for money or any future benefit. Do it because of the joyful desire to serve those you love, which means virtually everyone you meet. Such a mental attitude on its own can fill your life with prosperity and love. Just remember that the most excellent source of love is YOU!

## Minimalist Living

In this section, we will go over why you might want to consider becoming a minimalist and the many benefits that derive from it. Of course, this entire book is about living the minimalist lifestyle and to be therefore able to declutter your mind for the best.

Minimalism can be defined merely as a way to put a stop to the greed of the world around us. It's the opposite of every advertisement we see plastered on the radio, TV or the web. We live in a society that prides itself on the accumulation of stuff; we are fed up with consumerism, obsess about material possessions, accumulating debt, dwelling on distractions and never-ending noise. What we don't seem to have is any meaning left in our world as we know it.

By adopting a minimalist lifestyle, you can start by throwing out what you don't need to focus on what you do need. I know firsthand how little we need to survive. I was fortunate enough to live in a van for four months while traveling throughout Australia. This experience taught me many valuable lessons about what matters and how little we need from all this stuff we surround ourselves with.

# Less is more

Living a minimalist lifestyle is all about reducing what can be reduced. There are a few obvious benefits such as less cleaning and stress, a more organized household, and more money to be found, but there are also a few broad, life-changing benefits. What we don't usually realize is that when we reduce, we reduce a lot more than just stuff. If anything, the constant struggle of accumulating more and more things is a particular path to mind cluttering. Studies have shown that after a certain level of satisfaction is achieved when buying something; there is an absolute decrease in satisfaction that eventually tends to get to zero. The economists call it marginal satisfaction. The most common example they use to explain this concept is easy to grasp: think about the most fantastic cake you can imagine. Before you have it, you are susceptible to manifest a strong desire to eat that cake. After the first bite, you feel a great deal of satisfaction. The second taste can keep a high level of comfort but at some point the pleasure you feel from eating the cake slowly decreases. When you buy the same cake for the second time, a much lower degree of satisfaction is to be expected. The same happens with all possessions, no matter the origin.

The power of advertising makes it, so it is almost impossible for an individual to resist the urge of buying more and more things. They sell the projected satisfaction you will feel, but they never follow-up after you buy the product.

# Make space for what's vital

When we cleanse our garbage drawers and storage rooms, we make space, and we likewise interface with an outright peace. In the event that I would pick a correlation, the one that comes close by, and that I likewise alluded to in the early on a section of this book is the carousel. The jumbling wonders happen when we neglect to oppose the powerful stream of our general public, and we take part in this extreme and exhausting beat of steady purchasing with less and less fulfillment and point of view. In the event that we prepare for what is essential, accepting we discharge what that is, we lose that claustrophobic inclination, and we can inhale once more. Make a place to top off our lives with importance rather than stuff is a standout amongst the most proficient approaches to clean up and put a conclusion to self-depletion.

# More flexibility

The steady and nonstop collection of stuff resembles a stay; it secures us and indicates the weight we feel consistently. Envision you labor for three months and spare cash to purchase a costly device. Subsequent to getting a charge out of it for quite a while, not exclusively does the fulfillment you get from it diminishes, yet there's another advancement that emerges – we get connected to that protest, and we gradually, however, most likely build up the dread of losing it. On the off chance that we are straightforward, we understand that we are constantly frightened of losing our 'stuff.' Manage to release it, and you will encounter opportunity more than ever: flexibility from voracity, obligation, fixation and workaholic behavior. Much more thus, odds are the jumbling can't sneak in that effectively.

## Concentrate on wellbeing and pastimes

When you invest less energy at Home Depot attempting unsuccessfully to stay aware of the Joneses, you make an opening to do the things you adore, things that you never appeared to have time for. Also, the illustrations are such a large number of we could compose a completely new book just by assembling cases of dawdled doing fantastically insignificant things. We as a whole have been there, furtively wishing the 24 hour day would change into a 48 hour one, only for us, without any other person to know. In any case, at that point, if that would turn out to be valid, who could ensure that we wouldn't at present invest all the energy we have done a wide range of unimportant things that, at most, give us the dream that we can rest easy.

Everybody is continually saying they don't have enough time, yet what a number of individuals stop and take a gander at what they are investing their energy doing? It's to some degree clever, yet it appears that there is no time just to wrap up. You could appreciate a day with your children, hitting up the rec center, rehearsing yoga, perusing a decent book or voyaging. Whatever it is that you cherish you could do, however rather you are stuck at Sears looking for more stuff. Disappointing, would it say it isn't?

# Concentrate Less on material belonging

All the stuff we encircle ourselves with is just a diversion, and we are filling a void. Cash can't purchase satisfaction; we as a whole know the colloquialism. In any case, it can purchase comfort. After the underlying delight is fulfilled, that is the place our fixation on cash should end. Tragically, that is decisively where everything starts, for it is, for the most part, an exemplary instance of getting tied up with a fanciful solace. How about we understand this from with a better point of view. Envision you are eager. At that point, envision your mind believes that you ate, however, your body doesn't get the nourishing substances it needs. For quite a while, in light of the dream that happens inside your psyche, you don't feel hungry any longer. After that hallucination breaks, and they all do in the long run, do you feel hungrier than some time recently, as well as chances are you now feel wiped out, depleted, and drained? The same occurs with the deceptive filling of the void a considerable lot of us think.

It's hard not to get reserved into the consumerism trap. I additionally require steady updates that it's every one of the misguided feelings of joy. I have minutes when I appreciate stuff, however, I additionally perceive that I needn't bother with them,

We are barraged by the media displaying guarantees of satisfaction through material measures. Their instruments and abilities are significantly further developed than we might suspect they are. Furthermore, morals aren't the solid purpose of this area. In this manner, it's no big surprise we battle each day. The best counsel is to oppose those desires, despite the fact that it appears to be hard. In the event that we as a whole understand this is a vacant way that won't make us cheerful, we have a decent beginning stage.

## More significant serenity

When we stick to material belonging, we make pressure since we are constantly perplexed about losing these things. By rearranging your life, you can lose your connection to these things and at last make a quiet, serene personality.

The fewer things you need to stress over, the more peace you have, and it's as straightforward as that.

# More joy

While cleaning up your brain and your whole life, joy normally comes since you float towards the things that issue most. From being this last apparently inaccessible objective, satisfaction changes into an undeniable conclusion. You see the false guarantees that live in all the messiness, and you have an inclination that you have at last broken the shield against life's actual substance.

You will likewise discover satisfaction in being more productive, you will see a focus by having refocused your needs, and you will see happiness by appreciating backing off your pace and cadence.

# Less dread of disappointment

When you take a gander at Buddhist priests, they have no uncertainty, and they have no uncertainty since they don't have anything to lose, nor to pick up, so far as that is concerned

In whatever you wish to seek after you can exceed expectations on the off chance that you aren't tormented by the dread of losing all your common belonging. Clearly, you have to find a way to put a rooftop over your head, yet in addition, realize that you have little to fear aside from fear itself. The jumbling, as we settled as of now, feast upon our worry, and there are few to no psychological systems that could help us in such a manner. What helps, as we continue expressing all through the book, is learning, mindfulness, and point of view. In the event that anything, valor is developed by getting to this specific know-how and never releasing it.

## More Certainty

The whole moderate way of life advances singularity and confidence. By the by, it doesn't energize independence, self-centeredness, the expansion of one's sense of self. These days, an ever-increasing number of individuals get captured in this example that builds up the sense of self and thinks little of others. Genuine trust in yourself has nothing to do with decreasing others. Despite what might be expected. As expressed unmistakably in a past section of this book, helping other people and attempting to benefit them to the best of your capacities is simply the way certainty. This accepted exertion of situating towards others will make you more sure about your quest for bliss.

## Keep, toss, offer, give.

Experience your closet, your books, even your recollections and settle on this: what you're keeping, what you're discarding, what you're offering, and what you're giving.

Garments, for instance, anything that hasn't been worn for a long time, ought to go into one of the classifications said above.

Endeavor to locate a higher reason for this activity, something that will additionally persuade you. The demonstration of providing for the ones that are not as lucky, as a gift to philanthropy is the best choice out there.

Enter second-hand bunches on the web, possibly compose a carport deal for every one of your companions. On the off chance that the thing is too out designed, complete a correct deed and give it to somebody who has some expertise in making new, useful garments for those in require from the material of old garments.

After you dispose of the garments you don't wear, sort out your closet and bode well upbeat by appreciating the outcome – it is at long last the finish of the ceaseless tumult in your storage room.

You never thought it was conceivable, did you?

As the case presents itself, one of the indications of psyche jumbling that I find more frequently than I might want to concede is this: individuals get sincerely connected to things. The idea of enthusiastic esteem is orbiting the way we connect a few items with what they look like, or with what sort of memory it influences us to review.

A standout amongst the most charming yet commonsense answers for this issue introduced itself to me while having a discussion about this subject with an old man I met at a craftsmanship presentation, numerous years back. He was recording words like what labels or watchwords are, these days, on the web, in his notepad.

At the point when, sooner or later, I enquired him about his training, he revealed to me that he makes recollections by affiliation. Maybe a couple words for each work of art he loved, maybe a couple words for each workmanship question he adored. He said this is his one of a kind method for following his enthusiasm for gathering stunning bits of craftsmanship.

I was dazed by his vision, and I would always remember his notepad which appeared to be amazingly important.

## Discover your direction

There are numerous manners by which you could, inevitably, begin strolling the way to a moderate living style. One thing is certain, however: as you do it, the beneficial outcome it has at the forefront of your thoughts increments exponentially. A little space toward the start is gradually however clearly going to end up plainly a gigantic arrangement of opportunity at last.

Being free from the oppression of belonging is a flat out a way to your mind's cleaning up the process, and hence I ask everybody to in any event attempt this undertaking to see

# Conclusion

Thank you again for purchasing this book!

I hope this book was able to teach you the habits, actions, and mindsets you can use beat stress and clean up the mental clutter that might be holding you back from being more focused and mindful.

The next step is to put into practice what you read in this book because you'll find that this book is full of exercises that can have an immediate, positive impact on your mindset.

In other words, you should find a "quick win" that will have an immediate impact on your life.

Thank you and good luck!

Chloe S

# Happiness Advantage

––––– ✺❧✺ –––––

*Be Your Better Self and Achieve
Success Through Happiness*

**Chloe S**

# Introduction

I want to thank you and congratulate you for purchasing the book, *"Happiness Advantage"*.

This book contains proven steps and strategies on how to "Be your Better Self and Achieve Success through Happiness".

The research into happiness over the last 30 years has deepened our insight into what it means to be happy and how to achieve happiness. Recently, the research has shown that happiness is not a result of success but that in fact the opposite is true.

Happiness leads to success.

Drawing on a large number of studies that explore happiness and success, this book seeks to draw out some of the practical lessons so that you can choose your own happiness.

Learning techniques to become happier will help you enjoy life more and help you achieve your goals! Get started today and you'll see results within weeks.

Thanks again for purchasing this book, I hope you enjoy it!

# Chapter 1:
## Happiness and success

Conventional wisdom states that to be happy we need to have a successful career, a loving family, a good income and a healthy body. Consequently, many of us spend our lives chasing that smiling carrot that always seems to be just out of reach.

- If I lose a little weight, I'll be happy.

- If I get that promotion, I'll be happy.

- If I find the perfect partner, I'll be happy.

- If I get better grades, I'll be happy.

But it turns out that, in fact, the link between happiness and success is the other way around.

Happiness drives success

"Your brain at positive performs significantly better than at negative, neutral or stressed," says Shawn Achor in his massively successful Ted Talk on the *Happy Secret to Better Wor.*

Research study after research study has proven that the key to success is being happy.

When we are happy we are more creativity, energetic, productive, efficient and resilient. A positive attitude helps us deal with stress in a constructive way and allows us to see difficulties as challenges, not threats.

This is because, while negative emotions, like fear, narrow our focus and limits our actions (so that our ancestors could get away from tigers and bears without being distracted), positive emotions make us open to possibilities and new ideas. At the same time, positive emotions help us recharge and develop our personal resource.

# What is happiness?

When experts talk about happiness, what do they mean? Is the guy at the office who always clowns around happy? Is the mom at school who exudes calm and peace happy? Are you happy?

Barbara Fredrickson is one of the early positive psychology researchers. She started her research into positive emotions in the late '90s and has broken down positivity into "the big 10 emotions", namely: love, joy, gratitude, serenity, interest, hope, pride, amusement, inspiration and awe. In some sense happiness, (or as Frederickson prefers to call it "positivity"), is a combination of some or all of these emotions.

In their research, many academics define happiness to mean when a person has "satisfaction and meaning in their life". It's not a passing emotion, rather it's an inclination to feel positive emotions like "the big 10". It's also about being able to recover quickly from negative emotions.

Psychiatrist Manfred Spitzer says, "Long-term happiness has a lot to do with purpose and meaning and very little with consumption or gratification."

So are you happy? Are you more or less happy than you were last month? Are you happier than your neighbor?

These questions are difficult to answer because happiness is inherently subjective. No-one can really compare your experience of happiness to anyone else's.

It's true that there are some objective measures of happiness; the levels of cortisol in your body for example, which areas of your brain are seen to be active in a brain scan, or how many times you smile in a given period of time. Scientists use these indicators when conducting happiness studies, but for the most part they rely on how participants say they feel.

So how happy are you? And do you practice happiness skills in your daily life?

There are various online tools, questionnaires and mobile apps that can help you gauge your own level of happiness and any change in your positive state. For example, the organization Pursuit of Happiness has a skills quiz to test your daily happiness practices. Dave Sze at the Huffington Post explains how to track your own subjective wellbeing over time. Or you could try the Tactics for Happier Living quiz.

Researchers often try to measure what they call "subjective well-being". This usually involves asking people a range of questions that help the researcher understand their level of life satisfaction and their emotional experience.

To develop understand different aspects of happiness and develop reliable insights, researchers need to explore happiness using different methods. If studies using different research techniques all come to the same conclusion, then you can be fairly certain that the conclusions can be relied on.

Researchers in various disciplines, including psychology, psychiatry, economics and other health sciences, have designed studies to explore positivity, each study providing a little more insight into happiness, how it's experienced, what causes it and how you can create it.

Studies into happiness can be broken into four major types, which tend to observe or measure different aspects of happiness:

- Observation & experience sampling studies look at how people feel at a specific moment.

- Cross-sectional/correlation studies survey how people say they feel at one moment in time by answering various questions.

- Longitudinal studies are used to observe people's lives over time to find the trajectory of a happy life.

- Experimental studies try to find causal links between happiness and outside sources.

The positivity studies that have adopted these methods are starting to show a rich and nuanced understanding of the interplay between happiness, physical changes in the body and the brain, and behavior. We are starting to see how happiness forms part of a complex system.

While there are still many aspects of happiness that we don't fully understand, there are some key conclusions that are now well-accepted. That happiness precedes success and predicts success is one of these.

# Make yourself happy

It's all good and well understanding that happiness leads to success. But what if I'm just not a particularly happy person? Am I doomed to live a life of mediocrity? The good news is that happiness is something that we can all work on.

To some degree your level of happiness is determined by your DNA and your circumstances, but to a surprising degree, your happiness depends on you. As psychologists have come to understand what characteristics and behaviors help people to be happy, they have devised programs and advice to help people take control of their own happiness. And consequently, their own success.

So now, instead of putting all our energy into trying to be more successful, we need to start looking at how to be happier. We spend a great deal of time and effort making sure that our CVs are professional, that our projects are completed on time, and that we network with the right people. It's time to shift some of that effort to making ourselves happier.

Through this book, you will learn techniques and strategies that you can implement from day-to-day to make you a more positive person. And as you internalize a positive attitude, your behaviors in all areas of your life will change for the better.

Don't be daunted! While a few of the techniques we'll be looking at involve a level of long-term commitment and perseverance, many are so quick and easy to do that you can do them during your commute to the office, or while you're packing away your groceries.

You will also see the results quickly. Keep the perfect journal, and in just five days you can feel the difference. Take on the 21-day happiness advantage challenge and you experience sustained happiness within a month.

But before we look at how you can create your own happiness, let's look a bit deeper into what happiness looks like amongst successful people.

# Chapter 2:
# The Happiness advantage

Apart from the fact that happiness makes us, well, happy, there are numerous other benefits to be enjoyed.

You see, happiness triggers chemical processes in our bodies (dopamine and serotonin release) that prime the learning centers of our brains and make us more open to new experiences and information. A happy brain is better able to organize new information, store that information and make it easier to retrieve later. It is also better able to make neural connections. These connections speed up our processing powers, turn on our creativity, help us become more analytical, aid us in problem solving, and enable us to see things in a new and innovative ways.

As various authors have noted, happy individuals are successful across multiple life domains, including marriage, friendship, income, work performance, and health. Happy people are physically and mentally healthier, more successful at learning and work, more creative, more popular, more sociable, less likely to be criminal or addicted, and they live longer. Happiness makes people more sociable, more altruistic, better able to resolve conflict, healthier, and more accepting of themselves. Happy people are less egoistic, less aggressive, less abusive to others and less prone to illness.

# Happiness Benefits

"More than any other element, fun is the secret of Virgin's success."

*-   Richard Branson*


There is a very wide range of possible success outcomes when you are happy. But what does it mean to say, for example, "Happiness will make you more successful at learning"?

Let's unpack some of these outcomes in more detail to get a better understanding of just how big an impact happiness can have on our lives.

## Happiness boosts productivity and performance

Let's start in the workplace.

Various studies have been done to determine just how much more productive, effective and efficient a happy worker is than his or her peers.

In one productivity study, volunteers who ate chocolate and watched a funny video completed 10-12% more math problems that volunteers who watched a neutral video beforehand (without any delicious snacks).

Another study, by renowned positivity psychologist Martin Seligman, showed that happy employees are more likely to get better performance evaluations and higher pay.

A 15-year-long study of young people showed that happier participants were more likely to have gainful employment and higher income.

What's more happy employees have lower medical costs, work more efficiently and are absent less often.

In his book *Happiness Advantage*, Shawn Achor reports from studies his team have done that,

"When the human brain is positive ... Productive energy rises by 31 percent. The likelihood of promotion rises by 40 percent. Sales rise by 37 percent."

It's useful to note that in the context of productivity studies, you need to distinguish between happiness meaning personal well-being, and job satisfaction. The research into job satisfaction and productivity has very mixed results.

## Happiness improves learning

Happiness and learning have a wonderful, mutual relationship. Learning new things can help you become happier, and when you are happier you are better able to learn.

Studies have shown that there is a link between happiness and Grade Point Average (GPA) for students. Why would this be?

Imagine a classroom of students, anxious, withdrawn, and disengaged. These learners are essentially in a fight or flight mode. Their brains are in a narrow, guarded state. This is not the mode for learning.

Bring some fun and happiness into the class, and the learners adopt a more positive attitude. The brain abandons its threat response, dopamine levels increase, and a very special part, deep down in the center of the brain, activates.

This is the *nucleus accumbens*. Whether it's chocolate, exercise, laughter, friendship or sex, positive emotions make your *nucleus accumbens* light up.

In the 1950s, experiments showed that rats would push a button to stimulate this part of their brain to the exclusion of all other activity, including eating and sleeping. They ultimately died because nothing else was as satisfying as pushing that button.

For a long time, no-one understood what the purpose was of this part of the brain. We know that positivity activates it, but why? We now know that it is linked to learning. When the *nucleus accumbens* is activated we learn better, and because we are learning in a positive environment, we learn about the things that are good for us.

A positive brain broadens the number of possibilities we process, makes us more thoughtful, creative and open to new ideas. This allows us to develop intellectual, social and physical resources for the future. Positivist psychologist Barbara Fredrickson has termed this the "Broaden and Build Theory."

Dr. David Rock, co-founder of the NeuroLeadership Institute puts it like this,

"There is a large and growing body of research which indicates that people experiencing positive emotions perceive more options when trying to solve problems, solve more non-linear problems that require insight, [and they] collaborate better and generally perform better overall."

Happiness not only improves our ability to learn, we can also use learning to boost our happiness. This is because the *nucleus accumbens* isn't interested in the familiar. It wants new and exciting stimulus.

In the section on techniques to make yourself happier, you'll find out more about how to use learning to promote positivity.

## Happiness fosters creativity

In the same way, that positivity supports learning, it also supports creativity.

Researchers from the University of Toronto, exploring the link between happiness and creativity, used specially selected music to affect the participants' mood. Then they asked them to do two tests. The group of happy participants were better able to solve the creativity puzzle, than the other groups. However, the happy participants were less successful on the other task which required single-minded focus.

Researcher Adam Anderson explains, "With positive mood, you actually get more access to things you would normally ignore ... Instead of looking through a porthole, you have a landscape or panoramic view of the world."

Harvard researchers have similarly also found that creativity is less likely to be present with negative emotions such as fear, anger, sadness, and anxiety. Instead it is associated with positive emotions such as joy, love, and curiosity.

## Happiness improves health

There are numerous ways in which happiness promotes physical health. Daisy Coyle at HealthLine has summarized some of the evidence.

Firstly, happiness supports healthier lifestyle choices, like eating more healthily and getting more exercise.

- Adults who are happier have been found to be 47% more likely to eat fresh fruits and vegetables than less positive adults.

- Happy people are also 33% more likely to be physically active.

- Happy people have far fewer sleep problems than people with low levels of positive well-being.

Happiness has also been shown to boost the immune system, helping you fight off infections. For example, a study which exposed volunteers to the rhino and influenza viruses, found that volunteers with a positive emotional style were much less likely to contract the virus than their less happy counterparts.

Happiness reduces your stress levels. A number of studies have found that happier people have lower levels of cortisol (the stress hormone) in their bodies. In a stressful moment, happy people produce less cortisol and this effect seems to persist over time.

A positive attitude reduces your blood pressure and in so doing protects your heart. Various studies have found that happiness is linked to lower blood pressure and also to lower risk of heart disease. However the evidence is mixed and further research is needed in this area.

Believe it or not, happiness can actually help reduce pain. Studies into arthritis and stroke recovery have shown that people with positive well-being may experience less pain.

And to top it all off, a positive outlook can lead to a longer life. A number of large scale studies have shown a distinct link between happiness and greater life expectancy. One study involving 32 000 people found that unhappy individuals were 14% more likely to die during the 30 year-long study than happy ones.

# Chapter 3:
# Characteristics of happy people

Shawn Achor is a positivity psychologist who has studied people's happiness for years at Harvard University. His research has been key in showing that success follows happiness and not the other way around. His Ted Talk and book "The Happiness Advantage" have been massively popular and have made choosing happiness the talk of the town.

His numerous studies have shown that successful people share three key characteristics. According to Achor's studies these characteristics account for 75% of people's success in the workplace. Intelligence and technical skills make up the remaining 25%.

Achor notes, "If we can get somebody to raise their levels of optimism or deepen their social connection or raise happiness, turns out every single business and educational outcome we know how to test for improves dramatically."

So what are these amazing characteristics that we should all strive for?

- An optimistic outlook

- Perceiving an obstacle as a challenge not a threat

- Social connections

And while it's not easy to just through off your old ways and adopt a new positive approach, it is possible to shift your level of optimism, learn how to see challenges differently and build your social connections.

# Optimism

> "A pessimist sees the difficulty in every opportunity; an optimist sees the opportunity in every difficulty."
>
> *-- Winston Churchill*

**Are you a glass half full, or a glass half empty person?**

An optimistic person sees the glass as half full and approaches the world with hope and confidence, always expecting a favorable outcome. This doesn't mean that they are naïve or blind to possible risks, but rather that they view and plan for these in a positive way.

Research shows that there are enormous benefits to being optimistic. People this kind of outlook tend to:

- be healthier and live longer,

- be happier,

- be more resilient,

- better performance.

And while optimism has been shown to help protect against depression and various medical problems, like heart disease, pessimism has been linked with mood disorders, stress, and anxiety.

In some ways optimism is a self-fulfilling prophecy. If you expect people to like you, people are more likely to like you. If you expect a negotiation to go well, you are more likely to be happy with the result.

But don't confuse a positive view of the future with blind faith. Just believing in a wonderful outcome will not make it magically appear.

Contrary to popular belief, visualizing your dream outcome is not going to make it happen. There is a large body of research that shows that only visualizing your ideal in fact has the opposite effect. People who rely on visualization don't put in the effort needed to make things happen.

Similarly standing in front of the mirror and repeating upbeat mantras is not going to make you more optimistic.

Don't worry though, there are proven techniques that can help you shift to a more positive frame of mind.

**Learn to see problems as fleeting, limited and not your fault.**

To train yourself to be more optimistic you need to adjust the way you see each situation.

If something bad happens, do you always think it was your fault? When you encounter a setback, do you think that it's going to hold you back forever? When things don't go your way, do regard it as a giant catastrophe that is going to affect every area of your life?

If you're a pessimist then you probably answered yes to all these questions. Optimists on the other hand, tend to look at a negative situation and think that bad things are temporary, have specific causes, and are not their fault (at least not entirely).

And when good things happen, optimists perceive the positive situation as being long lasting, far reaching and brought about by their own actions. While pessimists think that good things are fleeting, rare and random.

To move from one camp into the other, the trick is to listen to the voice in your head that tells you that a negative event is a total disaster (pervasive) that it will last forever (permanent) and that it is all your fault (personal). Turn that story upside down!

The voice in your head says, "I've messed up and everybody is furious with me and now I am never going to get a promotion!"

Ask yourself: Is absolutely everybody really furious at you? Is this one mistake really going to outweigh all the good work you've done in the past? Was it entirely your fault?

It's sometimes useful to imagine someone else standing in your shoes. If your colleague was in this situation, would you really tell them that it was all their fault and that the consequences would be long term and catastrophic?

Probably not. We are better able to view events in an objective light when we are not directly involved. So do a little thought experiment and take yourself out of the equation. Every time you hear that negative self-talk, try to put the situation into perspective and adopt a more optimistic attitude.

# Seeing challenges not threats

A specific optimistic trait that happy people share is that they tend to redefine stress as a challenge rather than as a threat, and face demanding situations constructively and with a positive attitude.

These people see challenges as an opportunity to learn, grow, improve or change, and this has a number of positive consequences. First off, they feel less stressed because the situation is not a threat. They are also better able to address the challenge because they can put it into context. And they grow as they adapt and improve to deal with different situations.

Good news, as with developing a more optimistic attitude, you can retrain your brain to perceive challenges in a more positive way. Work on changing your approach, persevere and you'll not only become better at dealing with difficult situations, you'll also be more predisposed to being happy.

**Change how you react to challenges**

How do you react when a something bad happens? Your immediate reaction to any problem can lead you down a negative road. If you train yourself to change how you respond to and perceive problems, you can find better solutions and manage your stress levels at the same time. Jayson DeMers has some advice to help you shift your attitude towards problems.

**Remember that problems are part of life**

We encounter problems all day, every day. Some are so small that they barely register as a blip on the radar. Others are so predictable that they don't phase us. It's the problems that are a surprise or which are intense which really bother us. Remind yourself that you encounter and deal with problems all day. They are an unavoidable part of life. And remember that you are not alone. Everyone has problems, the only difference is how they deal with them.

**Don't jump to conclusions.**

As soon as we are faced by a problem, our brains want to jump to conclusions about the impact of that problem. If your car breaks down, you might immediately think that you are going to be late for work, that you are going to have to spend a lot of money to get it fixed, or that the kids are going to have to miss their dance classes.

**Stop these voices in their tracks!**

A broken down vehicle is just a broken down vehicle. Instead of jumping to conclusions, just describe the situation to yourself. "My car has broken down."

It's not easy, so start small and work your way up.

**Pretend it's happening to someone else.**

Remember in the section on how to train yourself to become more optimistic, you challenged your negative self-talk by asking yourself, "Would I say that to someone else?" To see challenging situations more objectively, you can try a similar trick.

Pretend that it's someone else in the situation. Your computer has just crashed! What kind of response would you have if this happened to a colleague? "Sarah's computer just crashed and she needs to call IT. Meanwhile she can access her mail and documents on her tablet."

Now you can see the situation more objectively and keep some of your heightened emotion at bay. If you can manage your emotional reaction to the situation, you can better see what you actually have control over and what the various options are for addressing it.

**How bad is it really?**

Once you've managed to see the situation a little more objectively, you can ask yourself how bad the consequences are really likely to be. You sent an email to the wrong person. Oops. But how serious is that really? Try listing all the possible negative outcomes that could result from your mistake. This helps you see not only the worst case scenario but the many other possible (and probably more likely) outcomes.

**Choose to add a positive spin.**

Try not to only react to the problem. I have a problem; now I need to fix it. Instead try to think of current or future improvements you can make. Instead of "My phone screen cracked; I need to take it for repairs," you could perhaps see the situation like this. "My phone screen cracked; this is a great opportunity to finally upgrade my handset." Keep practicing and eventually it will become more intuitive and you'll see the opportunities in each situation automatically.

Once the challenge is done and dusted, continue to control the narrative. Try to remember this experience in terms what you learned and how you benefited rather than the struggle itself. Also, think about the strength and skill that you needed to bring to bear to get past the challenge.

**Learn to use stress to your advantage**

Like problems, stress is an unavoidable part of life. We seem to be permanently under stress. Intense, unrelenting stress.

Stress is unhealthy when we use all our resources and don't have time to recover. We evolved the stress response to help us deal with acute stresses, but afterwards we need to rest and recover. When you feel constantly under threat, your body is operating in fight or flight mode without time to calm down and relax. That's when stress can lead to negative health and social consequences, like heart disease or divorce.

However, recent research shows that you shouldn't stress about stress. In fact you can use stress to your advantage and it can have a positive impact on your productivity and performance.

You're at the podium ready to speak to a room full of people. Your hands are sweaty. There are butterflies in your stomach. Your heart is pounding.

Just because you are feeling symptoms of stress (unpleasant as they may be), you don't need to see stress as an immediate problem. Instead of using your precious time at the podium trying desperately to calm down, you can make it work for you.

Since most of us (a resounding 91% in fact) don't deal with stress very well, it's encouraging to know that there are things you can do to improve your stress reaction. Changing your stress reaction will take time though, so be patient with yourself.

**Our bodies react to stress for a reason**

Remember that this stress response is there for a reason. We have evolved a stress response to better equip our bodies to deal with challenging situations. So instead of being disconcerted by your jitters, remember that your body is actually freeing up energy for you to use. Embrace it.

**Reach out**

Ever heard people talk about how bonding a stressful experience was? This isn't just because they've worked together to overcome the odds. When you get stressed, your body actually releases oxytocin, a chemical that helps us bond with other people. Use your stress advantage to connect with others. Make your team stronger.

And make yourself stronger. Research shows that talking to others about challenges helps us to connect to the people around us, and also correlates to having more friends and close colleagues, as well as greater happiness.

## Learn from your experience

You've said your speech, the audience applauded, the world did not end. Lying in bed, you replay the scene over and over and over in your head. You are focused on the stressful experience instead of being happy that it's over. But that's OK, you can make it work for you. Instead of just replaying the scene, and feeling stressed about it, really analyze the situation and learn from it.

# Social connections

"We are happy when we have family, we are happy when we have friends and almost all the other things we think make us happy are actually just ways of getting more family and friends."

-- Daniel Gilbert

One of the strongest recurring themes in positive psychology is the fact that people with high happiness scores have strong social connections.

In fact, social support is the greatest predictor of long-term happiness.

For example, a 2002 study at the University of Illinois found that the happiest students studied all shared the same characteristic. They had strong connections to their friends and family and committed significant effort to spending time with them.

Various other studies have shown that:

- People report being happiest when they are with their friends.

- People who are co-operative tend to be happier.

- Sharing personal feelings with others helps relieve stress and depression.

So happy people have strong relationships. And these aren't merely superficial relationships either.

Relationships that are the most beneficial are the ones where you feel comfortable sharing your feelings.

## Good relationships keep us happier and healthier

In 1938 a group of Harvard researchers wanted to find out more about what leads to a healthy and happy life. So they began an epic study. The researchers studied 258 male Harvard students with the intention of tracking them through their lives. Over time the group expanded to include the original recruits' children, and control groups were incorporated from other longitudinal studies.

The researchers studied the participants' health, relationships, life events and achievements. The participants were interviewed, their medical records examined, brain scans completed and behavior recorded.

And what did they find? Psychiatrist, Robert Waldinger, quips that the big take home message from the study is "All you need is love."

Waldinger expands on this, highlighting three lessons that they learned about relationships and health.

1. Social connections are really good for us. The men who reported close relationships were happier, physically healthier and lived longer than their counterparts. The participants were reported being lonely suffered negative consequences for their emotional, physical and mental health.

2. The quality of relationships is key. Participants whose marriages were stable and strong benefited.

While those whose marriages were fraught or high in conflict were in fact worse off than unmarried participants.

**3.** Strong, attached, supportive relationships protect or brains. Participants with felt they could count on their partner enjoyed better memory.

## The value of relationships

Researchers have tried to put a monetary value on the benefits that social connections bring and the costs that social disconnects entail. This quantifiable measurement of happiness allows us to compare different life events to see how much impact they really have in terms of life satisfaction.

Nattavudh Powdthavee, author of the "Putting a price tag on friends, relatives and neighbors" study worked out values for health, a better social life, marriage, seeing friends and family regularly, divorce, unemployment, separation, and death of a spouse.

Good health provides a large amount of life satisfaction and is valued at +$463,170. A better social life works out to +$131,232. Marriage is valued at +$105,000. Meanwhile unemployment amounts to -$114,248 and death of a spouse is like losing $308,780 per year.

The study concluded that "an increase in the level of social involvements is worth up to an extra £85,000 a year [app. $131 232] in terms of life satisfaction. Actual changes in income, on the other hand, buy very little happiness."

# Chapter 4:
# Be happy by choice not chance

Is it possible to work at being happy? Experts say yes!

While your genes and your environment will affect your happiness, you can do a surprising number of small and easy things in your daily life to make you happier.

We know that DNA plays a role in hour happiness. (Studies have found that identical twins are more likely to have similar happiness scores than fraternal twins.) However, researchers think that a large portion of our happiness is determined by our daily experiences. Sonia Lyubomirsky, for example, holds that 40% of our happiness is based on our day-to-day lives.

You see, the brain is amazingly flexible. It quickly learns new things and new ways of doing things. When you practice doing things repeatedly, your brain rewires itself so that each time you do that new thing, your brain can do it more efficiently and with less conscious effort. In essence, you create a new habit. And yes, you can create a happiness habit.

Shawn Achor notes that, "Happiness is a work ethic . . . . It's something that requires our brains to train just like an athlete has to train."

From the extensive body of research into happiness, a number of practical techniques have emerged. These handy tips really will help you to become happier. Luckily,

131

a surprising number of them don't take much time and are easy to integrate into your daily life.

The rest of this book is dedicated to the numerous techniques that the research as unearthed. While all the techniques outlined here have evidence to back them up, some are better established than others. The six that that have the most evidence are presented in detail up front. The remaining techniques have been compiled into a happiness shopping list for you to pick and choose from. Have fun!

# What strategies should you choose?

In his book *Happiness Advantage*, Achor promotes a five point happiness plan focused on gratitude, journaling, performing acts of kindness, exercise and meditation. He encourages people to try one of these techniques for 21 days to feel a real difference.

Richard Wiseman in *59 Seconds* proposes a few techniques from the body of research that can be done in less than a minute. These include smiling more, keeping the perfect journal for a week, and performing acts of kindness.

As you decided which techniques you'd look to try, bear this in mind. Don't just select the ones that will fit neatly and easily into your daily routine. To get the most out of these techniques, you really need to make an effort. So if exercise doesn't come that easily to you, you may well benefit more from going for a walk each day than you would from meditating.

# All you need is love

"Good relationships keep us happier and healthier. Period,"

*-- Robert Waldinger*

Many, many studies (like the long-term Harvard study discussed earlier) have shown that relationships are extremely important to happiness.

Forming and maintaining good relationships is hard work. It's not a quick fix, but has incredible long-term implications for your health and happiness. It's worth the effort.

## Listen actively

Many psychologists believe that to improve your relationships so that there is a deeper connection, you can work on listening carefully to your loved ones and responding in encouraging ways.

"Active listening" means that you are listening with all senses.

Actually pay attention to what people say. (Yes, that means put down your phone or look away from your screen.) And let them say what they want to say; don't interrupt or interject with your own opinion or anecdote. Ask them questions and encourage them to share.

It's important that the person you are speaking to is aware that you are paying full attention and really listening to what they are saying. Use eye contact. Nod your head.

Smile. Even saying "mmm hmmm" indicates that you are listening.

When someone knows you are really interested in what you are saying, they will feel more at ease and so communicate more easily, openly and honestly. This will help you create deeper relationships.

Here is a little experiment to try. Next time someone comes to you with a problem, be it personal or professional, put aside all distractions and give them all your attention. Encourage them to talk. Adopt open body language. Ask interested questions. (Avoid why questions that might sound judgmental.) Most important of all, don't try to provide an answer to the problem and don't pull the focus back to you by sharing your similar experiences.

## Share new experiences

Studies have shown that relationships benefit from new experiences and researchers seem to have had a great deal of fun designing experiments to test whether novelty really improves relationships!

Psychologist Arthur Aron and his team set up a lab experiment to test whether couples who were asked to do a new and challenging task together, felt better about their relationships than the control group. While one control group merely walked back and forth across the room, the other couples were asked to push a ball across the room with their arms and legs tied together. The study showed that the couples who did the challenging task reported feeling more love and better satisfied with their relationships than before the task.

So try new things.

For example, you could plan a trip together. Research shows that travelling with your friends or family can help strengthen relationships. These shared experiences can improve communications and improve well-being.

**Romantic relationship booster tips**

After synthesizing the research into how to improve your romantic relationship, Richard Wiseman advises that you keep a journal for three days.

On day one, he advises that you spend 10 minutes writing down your deepest feelings about your current relationship.

On day two, he says that you should spend some time thinking about someone whose relationship is inferior to your own. Then write down three important reasons why your relationship is better than theirs.

Finally, on day three, Wiseman says that you should note down the most the quality in your partner that you value the most and explain why it is so important to you.

A few minutes of writing over three days to boost your relationship. It certainly seems with a try.

**Take Action:**

Here are a few other ideas to help you strengthen some of the other relationships in your life.

- Really listen and pay attention.

- Replace screen time with people time.

- Refresh a stale relationship by doing something new.

- Reach out to a family member you haven't spoken to in years.

- Call a friend when you're not OK.

- Talk about your past: your family, your childhood, your first date, your first car.

- Always show up at birthdays, anniversaries or any other special occasion.

- Leave a note saying thank you.

# Gratitude

"We tend to forget that happiness doesn't come as a result of getting something we don't have, but rather of recognizing and appreciating what we do have."

*-- Fredrick Koeing*

It's no coincidence that self-help celebrities like Oprah Winfrey have locked onto gratitude journaling. Writing down the big and small things that you are thankful for each day, really does impact on your mood.

Numerous studies have been done into the impact of gratitude on well-being and reviews of the results show that there is an undeniable link between them.

- Gratitude will make you happier.

- It will improve your relationships.

- It can make life better for everyone around you.

- Feeling grateful will even make you feel more energized, alert, and enthusiastic.

Scientists believe that gratitude improves your happiness because you train your brain not to focus on the negative things around you but rather to see and appreciate the positive.

It's easy to take things for granted: the beautiful weather, a generous friend, a delicious meal, a roof over your head. When you actually take time to think about what you are thankful for each day, you bring these things back into mind and often re-experience the positive emotions that they created in you.

Gratitude is easy to incorporate into your life, it's beneficial to you and the person you thank, and it has a positive physical and psychological benefits. Just take a few minutes each day to write down a few things that you are grateful for. Easy as that.

Keeping a gratitude journal is an excellent way to help you focus on what you appreciate in your life. While you can express your gratitude in other ways, studies indicate that the act of writing seems to be an important factor in reaping the positive benefits of gratitude.

Need some inspiration? Here are some ideas to get you started.

- Find something in nature to be grateful for.

- Say thank you to the people who love you.

- Be grateful to the people who offend you.

- Be thankful for some aspect of your body and mind.

- Identify a routine in your life to be thankful for.

Remember to be specific about what you are grateful for.

If you don't want to keep a gratitude journal, there are other ways to write down what you are thankful for. Leave a quick post-it note or send a short email thanking people for doing things for you. Or if you'd prefer to go old school write a letter!

**Take Action:**

- Start a gratitude journal. List a few things you are grateful for every day.

- Tell people directly that you are grateful for what they have done for you and why.

- Take someone to lunch or buy them coffee.

- Leave a quick post-it note saying thanks.

- Write a letter to someone who means a lot to you or who has done something significant for you.

- Send an email every morning to someone who's done something you appreciate.

- Relive the memory of something for which you are particularly grateful.

- Post your grateful comments on social media.

# Journaling

Keeping a journal or diary can be a very powerful way to boost your mood. This is partly because the act of writing something down requires you to structure your thoughts leads you inherently to start thinking about a solution.

Researchers have documented numerous benefits from journaling, including drastic emotional benefits and physical health benefits.

What you write about matters, and different studies indicate that journaling is more or less effective based on the topic of the writing.

## Positive experience journaling

Achor advises that you describe one positive experience you had in the last day. "This is a strategy to help transform you from a task-based thinker, to a meaning based thinker who scans the world for meaning instead of endless to-dos."

## Negative experience journaling

Studies that asked participants to write daily journal entries detailing their deepest thoughts and feelings about a significant negative experience have found that their physical health, mood and self-esteem improved .

## Relationship venting

Writing about a break up can help you get over the failed relationship more quickly and will also help you build a stronger sense of self-identity after the break up.

## Ideal future

Although visualizing an ideal future won't make it happen, writing about it can make you happier. Participants in a study conducted by Laura King from the Southern Methodist University who described their ideal (but not unrealistic) future for four days running were significantly happier than the control groups.

## Appreciative writing

You've already discovered the enormous benefits that practicing gratitude holds in store. You can use your journal to write down a few things each day that you are grateful for. Alternatively, you can describe what you appreciate most in your romantic partner, friend or colleague.

## Affectionate writing

Writing an affectionate letter to someone you love can result in a significant increase in happiness. Studies have also found that it can lower your stress levels and even decrease your cholesterol levels!

## The perfect journal

Wiseman, having reviewed much of the research into journaling, has created a 5-day journal adopting many of the different elements that studies have shown to be effective. He's called this "the perfect journal".

This approach incorporates elements of positive journaling, gratitude, and kindness. Wiseman believes that if you keep this journal for just 5 days, you will already start to feel happier.

Day 1: List at least three things that you have been grateful for over the previous week.

Day 2: Choose an experience that you really enjoyed from your past and write about it. Imagine how you felt at the time.

Day 3: Imagine what your life would be like if you achieved all the things that are currently working for.

Day 4: Write a short letter to someone you care about explaining how much you care about them and their impact on you.

Day 5: Review the week and note three things that went really well, regardless of how trivial or momentous they were.

**Take Action:**

- Start writing today.

- You can write for anywhere between 2 and 20 minutes depending on what you want to write about.

- Keep a hand written journal, as this seems to be more effective than typing on a keyboard.

143

# Exercise

"Warning: Exercise has been known to cause health and happiness."

*-- Anonymous*


Have you ever noticed how exercise can utterly shift your mood? Start your run grumpy and you'll end it smiling. Drag yourself to the gym in the early morning, and you'll leave full of pep. This effect has been studied by numerous researchers who have found that there is a significant link between exercise and feeling happy.

Researchers have found various links to explain this. Firstly, there is a physiological basis for why physical activity makes you feel better; exercise releases endorphins and dopamine which are the feel good chemicals of the brain. Exercise is also often a social activity and the interactions with others can contribute to happiness.

Various studies have also found that exercise:

- increases your energy,

- improves your sleep,

- helps you be more creative,

- increases your productivity,

- improves your memory,

- helps you cope with challenges in a positive way, and

- increases your overall brain performance.

An extensive Cochrane Review of studies on exercise and depression has shown that there is compelling evidence that exercise is a significant way to combat depression.

In light of this evidence, experts recommend exercise as a good way to improve your happiness. Achor suggests that you exercise for 10 minutes a day, arguing that this will "train your brain to believe your behavior matters, which causes a cascade of success throughout the rest of the day." Other experts encourage you to aim for at least 30 minutes a day.

**Take Action:**

- Exercise from 10 minutes upwards each day.

- Choose an activity that is suited to your lifestyle and fitness level.

- To get a bonus happiness boost, exercise outdoors with someone else.

# Meditate and be mindful

"If you are quiet enough, you will hear the flow of the universe. You will feel its rhythm. Go with this flow. Happiness lies ahead. Meditation is the key."

-- Buddha

Many people who practice mindfulness or meditation report feeling more relaxed and better able to cope with daily stress. They experience a shift in reality. The world around them changes and becomes calmer and easier to navigate. While these experiences may sound religious or esoteric, there is also evidence to back them up.

## Meditation has dozens of benefits

*Psychology Today* collated some of the research results relating to meditation. These studies show that meditation:

- improves boosts your immune system

- reduces pain (better than morphine!)

- improves cardiovascular health

- decreases inflammation

- increases positive emotion

- decreases depression

- decreases anxiety

- decreases stress

- increases social connection and emotional intelligence

- makes you more compassionate

- makes you feel less lonely

- improves your self-control

- improves your ability to introspect

- increases your focus and attention

- improves your memory

- improves decision making

- can help you overcome addiction

Shawn Achor in his discussion of the Happiness Advantage states, "It's not necessarily reality that shapes us but that the lens through which your brain views the world shapes your reality." And studies into meditation seem to bear this out.

## Meditation physically affects our brains and bodies

Scientists have shown that people who practice mindfulness meditation actually have lower levels of stress hormone in their bodies after performing a stressful activity like public speaking than others who practice more conventional forms of stress management.

Other researchers have found that the brains of participants who took a Mindfulness-Based Stress

Reduction program for eight weeks physically changed. These changes were focused on the hippocampus, the area of the brain linked to regulating emotion, arousal, and responsiveness.

Researchers have even found that the relaxed state produced by meditation, yoga, and breathing exercises switches on genes that are related to augmenting our immune system, reducing inflammation, and fighting a range of conditions from arthritis to high blood pressure to diabetes.

Meditation also reduces the density of brain tissue associated with anxiety and worry, while it enhances the areas lined to mental processing and empathy.

## So start meditating

There are many different kind of meditation and finding the right one for you is important as research shows that the type of meditation you choose will affect whether you stick with it or not. You need to enjoy your meditation.

But don't be intimidated if you have never meditated before. There are many videos and guides online to help you, and a quantity of relaxation and meditation apps. But you don't even need these to get started.

## Take Action:

For a quick start into Mindfulness Meditation:

- Sit quietly and comfortably.

149

• Relax (or close) your eyes.

• Pay attention to your breathing.

• Whenever you get distracted, notice the thought or feeling and then let it go and return to the present.

• Bring your focus back to breathing.

• Start by meditating for a couple of minutes. You can extend this later.

# Perform acts of kindness

"If you want happiness for an hour, take a nap. If you want happiness for a day, go fishing. If you want happiness for a year, inherit a fortune. If you want happiness for a lifetime, help somebody."

*-- Chinese Proverb*


It is better to give than to receive. This sentiment has been shared across the ages by different cultures and beliefs.

Now we have the evidence to back up this ancient knowledge. Brain imaging shows that giving lights up the same areas of the brain as food and sex, implying that we have evolved to give and be kind.

Research also shows that spending money on others makes you happier than spending money on yourself. Giving donations to charities or buying gifts for others can boost your happiness significantly.

However, giving doesn't only refer to financial transactions.

Simply acts of kindness like writing a thank you note, donating to a food drive or helping someone change a tire will also make you feel happy.

Unfortunately there is a flip side to giving: being taking advantage of. To avoid this try to give to causes that you are passionate about. Give to effective and transparent charities. Offer your time rather than money. Volunteer -

don't wait to be asked. Don't let people guilt trip you into giving.

And, as it happens, acts of kindness are contagious. Do something kind for someone and they are likely to do something kind for someone else in return. In a sense, it's the pay it forward principle. When someone does something kind for you, you are prompted to do something kind as well.

There have been some fabulous examples in the past few years. In 2014 a Starbucks customer paid for the coffee of the next person in the queue. Instead of merely accepting this generosity, the next person paid for the person behind them, and so on for 11 hours and 378 customers!

Regularly do kind things regularly other people and you'll quickly experience a happiness shift. This does not mean that you need to make large donations to charities or volunteer hours and hours of your time. A few small non-financial acts of kindness every day will do wonder•s. Compliment someone. Get in touch with an old friend.

**Take Action:**

Try to do a few acts of kindness every day, the possibilities are endless!

- Send an email that compliments or appreciates someone.

- Say hello to the person next to you in the elevator.

• Help someone in passing, whether it's helping a mother carry her stroller up the stairs, or supporting an elderly person across the road.

• Drive kindly – give others space to merge into the lane, smile at other drivers.

• Leave a generous tip for a waiter with a note of thanks.

# Your happiness shopping list

Improving your social connections, being grateful, journaling, meditating and getting exercise are the big guns, but there are loads of other techniques that have all kinds of beneficial side effects, including happiness.

## Get a dog

"A person can learn a lot from a dog ... about living each day with unbridled exuberance and joy, about seizing the moment and following your heart ... about friendship and selflessness and, above all else, unwavering loyalty."

– John Grogan

There is a body of research that indicates that dog owners are happier, more satisfied at work and more sociable than people without a dog.

Researchers have found, for example, that dog owners who have had a heart attack have better recovery than those without a dog.

Studies also shows that dog owners cope well with daily stress, are more relaxed, have lower blood pressure in stressful situations and have high self-esteem. Experiments have even been done that show that having your dog in the room with you when you are doing a stressful task will lower your stress response.

What exactly is it about dogs?

It might be that dogs are the best non-judgmental friends around. It could be that you experience the positive benefits of touch when you stroke or pet your dog. Even looking into your dog's large, loving eyes will boost your happiness, as it raises the oxytocin levels in your brain.

Over and above all of these, walking your dog brings the benefits of exercise, being outdoors and engaging in social interaction into play:

- Dog owners are almost twice as active as non-dog owners.

- Dog owners are smiled at or approached by strangers far more often than other walkers.

- Dog owners take on average 2760 more steps per day than non-dog owners.

- Dog owners watch less TV than non-dog owners.

- Dog owners are likely to pursue outdoor hobbies and activities.

So if you are able to own and care for a dog, consider this as a super boost to your health and happiness. Unfortunately, while there is evidence to support the impact that cats have on health, there is little evidence to show that cats have the same impact on mood.

**Take Action:**

- Get a dog and give it a cuddle.

- Borrow a dog and take it for walk.

- Go up to someone walking their dog and engage them in conversation.

**Sleep well**

We all need to sleep well. Study after study has shown that adults typically need eight hours of sleep a night and that proper sleep is essential for our well-being.

* Sleep improves memory retention and learning new tasks.

* Inadequate sleep is associated with family issues, problems at school, physical health problems, and depression.

* Sleep deprivation is linked to obesity and diabetes.

* Sleep deprivation is also associated with impairments to memory, thinking speed, reaction time, and cognitive ability.

* Sleep deprivation is also linked to mood instability, over-reacting and poor judgment.

To boost your mood and your well-being you need to get a good night's sleep, every night. This means that you should get approximately eight hours of uninterrupted sleep, which is harder than it sounds.

**Take Action:**

Here are a few tips to help improve your sleep.

* Avoid caffeine in the five or six hours before bedtime

* Establish a bedtime routine.

- Ensure that your bedroom is dark and a comfortable temperature.

- Avoid spending time looking at a screen before bed time.

- Make sure you're tired – get enough exercise during the day.

- Keep the bedroom for sleep and sex.

## Get outside

A gorgeous mountain hike, a swim in a forest pool, diving a coral reef, it's common sense really: nature makes us happy (well, most of us). But did you know that a house plant can make you feel good? Or that trees can lower the murder rate in a city? The natural world really does improve people's well-being.

You don't need to travel to a tropical island or go on safari to reap the benefits of nature. Spend 15 minutes in your local park and you will already start to you feel psychologically restored.

There are in fact numerous benefits from spending time outdoors. First and foremost, researchers have found, in a number of studies, that getting outside makes people feel happier. In one experiment, researchers got people to take a walk. Half the participants walked for 50 minutes in an urban setting. The other half in a natural setting. The participants who walked out in nature experienced decreased anxiety, decreased rumination (running over things in your mind), and fewer negative emotions. They also maintained their positive attitude well and experienced improved working memory.

New technologies have allowed scientists to explore the link between space and attitude in exciting new detail. The Mappiness project captures in real time where people are and how they feel using a Smart phone app. Over 35 000 people have volunteered as part of the study. Researcher George MacKerron found that people are not happy at work, but are happy on vacation, with friends and listening to music. "They're also very, very happy when they are outside."

Additional positive mental benefits from spending time in nature include:

- Being outdoors reduces mental fatigue, broadens your thinking, improves your creative problem solving and improves your working memory.

- Being in nature decreases stress and anxiety, although the reasons for this are still largely unknown.

- Mother nature encourages you to be kind and generous .

- Being outdoors makes you feel more alive, even overcoming feelings of exhaustion.

Actually spending time out of doors is one thing, but researchers John Zelenski and Elizabeth Nisbet wanted to explore if how we feel about nature impacts on our happiness. Connectedness to nature is not a measure of how much time you spend in nature but rather how important being outdoors is to you, and whether you consider it an important part of yourself.

The researchers found that our emotional connectedness to nature is different from the other psychological connections in our lives, like our social or cultural connections. They also discovered that our connectedness to nature is a good predictor of happiness, regardless of other factors.

**Take Action:**

159

All this gives you an excellent reason to get outside:

- Plan a weekend trip to a nature reserve.

- Spend your lunch hour in the park.

- Instead of reaching for a cup of coffee to pep you up, step outside.

- Look out the wioondow or load nature scenes as the wallpaper on your computer.

## Enjoy the sun (in moderation)

Related to spending time outdoors, it seems a good dose of sunshine can also make us happier.

In fact, people who don't get enough sunshine can suffer from Seasonal Affective Disorder (SAD). Sometimes called "winter blues" this depressive disorder effects people when the days are shorter and there is less sunlight. It's been estimated that up to 20% of Americans are affected by Seasonal Affective Disorder (SAD) each winter. Sufferers experience low mood, low energy, irritability, difficulty concentrating, changes in eating patterns and, in some cases, more serious depression.

While the research into this area is not definitive, there are a number of theories as to why and how sunshine might make us feel happier.

• Research is emerging to show that low vitamin D levels are linked to low mood. Feeling sunshine on your skin helps your body to produce Vitamin D.

• Regular exposure to sunlight can increase your serotonin levels, making you more active and alert.Serotonin creation is triggered when sunlight hits the retina in the eyes. This is why full-spectrum light therapy works for people with SAD. Limited-spectrum artificial light doesn't have the same effect.

• Exposure to sunlight also results in a drop in melatonin, the chemical that our bodies produce to get us into a calm and relaxed state, ready for sleep. Too much melatonin might cause you to feel lethargic.

161

• Recent research has also posited a link between mood and the number of sunny hours in the day (regardless of the weather or pollution levels). The more sunny hours, the happier everyone feels.

There are additional benefits to getting sufficient sun. Studies have shown that as well as boosting your mood, sunshine (specifically vitamin D) may help prevent certain cancers. And it is an important component of your sleep cycle; each morning your cycle restarts with the sunrise. UV exposure also releases nitric oxide which lowers blood pressure.

Advice to enjoy the sun does, of course, need to be tempered by warnings to avoid the sun since, as we all know, too much sun has been linked to skin cancer. In fact, it's possible that sunscreen may be playing a role in the lower Vitamin D levels that doctors are finding. A more indoor lifestyle is probably also playing a role. So get out and enjoy the sun, in moderation.

**Take Action:**

• Take a 15 to 20 walk in the early morning sunshine without your sunscreen (when the chance of getting sunburned is low).

• Use your coffee and lunch breaks to have a sun break.

• Have your vitamin D levels tested, and if necessary get Vitamin D supplements.

• During dark, winter months if you feel the winter blues, use a full spectrum light box for 30 minutes a day.

## Buy experiences not stuff

"If more of us valued food and cheer and song above hoarded gold, it would be a merrier world."

– J.R.R. Tolkien

Can money buy happiness? The answer to this isn't actually as simple as you might think. Conventional wisdom says no, money can't buy happiness but a surprisingly large number of people still think that when they are rich (or richer) they will be happy.

Finding the rather complex answer to the money-happiness question started with research conducted in the late-1970s which concluded that money doesn't lead to happiness. Researchers studied lottery winners against other randomly-selected people. They found that there was no significant difference between the happiness levels of the two groups. Winning the Lottery didn't make people happier. The only real difference was that the people in the control group got more joy out of the small things in life.

Not only does an unexpected bonus not make you happy, even when people have obtained their wealth through their own effort, there still appears to be no link between money and happiness. It seems that when you get a salary increase or buy a new car, you only feel a short-lived burst of happiness. After a while the feeling passes and your new house or beautiful jewelry just becomes part of the status quo.

What's more, studies exploring materialism and happiness have shown that people who value possessions are likely to be less happy and less satisfied.

More recently, we've learn that money can buy happiness, up to a point. Researchers Kahneman and Deaton studied the happiness levels in families with varied incomes. They found that additional money in a family income below $75 000 does increase happiness. However, above this threshold the link between money and happiness ceases.

This is borne out at the country level. Poor countries (those with a low GDP) are typically less happy, but after a certain point, wealth is no longer a predictor of happiness.

To complicate this question even further, there actually are some things that you can spend money on that will increase your happiness.

1. Spend money on other people. Studies have consistently shown that people who send a higher percentage of their income on other people are happier than people who send their money on themselves.

2. Spend money to free up your own time. Researchers found that people who spend money to get others to do chores that they do not enjoy, thus freeing up their own time, feel more positive than those who don't.

The relationship between money and happiness can be summarized as follows. Money helps us become happier when it helps us meet our basic needs. Beyond that, money doesn't make us happy. More specifically, spending money on possessions does not make us happy. But spending money on experiences and other people does make us happier.

So go on holiday. Take a trip to the theatre. Go skydiving. Having new and interesting experiences will boost your happiness, especially if you share the experience with others (during and after).

What's more, give your loved one's experiences as gifts, and you'll spread the happiness around.

**Take Action:**

- Instead of saving up to buy yourself a luxury treat, decide to rather save up for an experience.

- Next time you give a birthday present, give an experience (a shared meal, a movie, learning how to kite surf, teaching someone how to make a much-loved dish).

## Smile

"Sometimes your joy is the source of your smile, but sometimes your smile can be the source of your joy."
— *Thich Nhat Hanh*

People smile when they are happy, but did you know that you can become happy because you are smiling?

Some rather odd experiments in the early 80's have shown that people who force their muscles into a smile (by holding a pencil between their teeth or saying "eeeee") start to feel happier.

The fact that these smiles aren't genuine doesn't seem to matter very much.

While the mechanism behind this effect is still not fully understood, there is one theory that smiling constricts veins in the face that would ultimately lead to a reduction in the amount of blood from the carotid artery to the brain.

However it happens, the effect seems to be real and we can exploit this interesting fact of biology to our own benefit.

This is probably the easiest technique to fit into your everyday routine. Just smile more. You don't even need to be smiling at someone or something. The simple act of pulling your facial muscles into a smile configuration will help you become happier.

Do try to make the smile as genuine as possible. Maybe think of something funny or endearing as you fake smile your way up the elevator. Also try to maintain the smile for 30 seconds if you can.

As you fake a smile to make yourself happier, you could well make someone else happier too. When you smile at someone, they will smile back. It's instinctive and unthinking. So you can use your smile to change your own mood, and make the world around you a happier place.

**Take Action:**

It's quite easy to forget to smile on purpose. So here are some ways to remind yourself.

- Smile at yourself whenever you look in a mirror.

- Associate something with smiling, like a color or word, and smile each time you see or hear it.

- Watch funny YouTube videos.

- Think of a happy memory.

- And if you're desperate, put a pencil between your teeth!

## Straighten your posture

Believe it or not, good posture will affect your mood and your performance!

Get students to sit up straight when they do a math test and you'll find that they do better and feel happier than their slouching counterparts. At least the students in the study conducted by researchers at Colorado Collage did.

Not only that, good posture can increase your energy levels, improve your confidence and reduce your fears. People even report that it is harder to remember negative memories when they stand or sit up tall.

How is this possible? Basically, the effect is psychological. When we're sad or miserable, we tend to lower our heads and slouch our backs. So we can basically trick our brains into feeling positive by adopting a tall, straight posture with chest out and chin up.

Good posture can improve your mood, so channel your mother's voice in the back of your head and stop slouching.

**Take Action:**

You can also try a few creative tricks to remind you.

- Stand against a wall with your head, shoulders and butt just touching the wall. This is what good posture feels like!

- Stick a post-it to your computer screen, reminding you to sit up.

• Associate a color with posture. Each time you see that color, sit up!

• Stand up straight. Get someone to put tape across your back from your left shoulder to your right hip, and from your right shoulder to your left hip. You'll feel the tape move if you start to slouch.

• Strengthen your core muscles doing stomach and back exercises.

• Put a photo or picture just higher than head height on the wall behind your desk so you have to look up to see it.

• Adjust your driving mirror so it's a bit higher so you have to sit taller while you drive.

## Take the good with the bad

It sounds rather counter intuitive but feeling mixed emotions together is another proven way to boost positivity. By now it's fairly well-understood accepted that we should express our emotions, both negative and positive. (Though doesn't appear to be practiced as widely as it should be.) But feeling positive and negative emotions and expressing them at the same time?

A number of studies have looked at the impact it has on participants when they acknowledge the complexity of life and embrace a wide range of emotions, good and bad. These studies show that mixed-emotional experiences improve well-being.

So when something bad happens, recognize your negative feelings but also try to see the bright side. This may take the sting out of negative experiences in the moment and can also have a lasting effect.

As a bonus, feeling negative and positive emotions together has also been found to improve health, specifically can reduce typical age-related decline.

**Take Action:**

- Don't suppress your negative feelings. Acknowledge them and then actively seek a positive angle.

- When you journal about a negative experience, also think about any positive outcomes.

# Keep your happy friends close

Research has shown that happiness is contagious. If you are surrounded by happy people you are more likely to be happy yourself.

A longitudinal study undertaken in Framingham, Massachusetts over three generations has shown that happiness moves through a population. In fact happiness is so contagious that it can even affect the friend of a friend of a friend.

This impact is even stronger if you are geographically close to your happy friends. Friends who live within a mile of you have a massive impact on your happiness (but not your level of sadness). Neighbors and family also effect on your happiness but not to the same degree.

**Take Action:**

- Engage with your happy friends and neighbors.

- Create connections with new people in your immediate community.

# Learn something new

Earlier, you read that happiness improves learning because it activates a center of the brain called the *nucleus accumbens*. When you are feeling positive emotions, your brain makes itself open to new experiences, and becomes better at retaining and analyzing information.

You can use this process to boost your happiness, your self-confidence, and your resilience by learning something new. A new challenge will also help you stay curious and engaged.

Learning a new skill may bring more stress in the short-term but will contribute to a greater daily sense of happiness later on. Researchers suggest that you can reduce the short-term stress by making sure that you choose what you want to learn (sense of autonomy) and do the activity with others if you can (social connectedness).

You don't have to achieve your ultimate goal to see the benefits and you don't need to engage in formal learning. Taking up a hobby, joining a club, or learning to play a sport will all bring you happiness as your brain revels in the novelty.

**Take Action:**

- Choose something you've always wanted to do and learn how to do it.

- Can you learn this with someone?

## Give up one of your favorite things

It sounds rather odd, but if you give up one of your favorite things for a few days it will actually increase your willpower and boost your happiness.

Think about it for a few seconds. When you've denied yourself chocolate for a few days, what do you do when you next have some? You don't scoff it down unthinkingly, you savor it. And that's the trick.

In a world of abundance, many of us are able to fulfil our wants and needs at virtually any time. We aren't often denied what we want. Denying ourselves the odd daily pleasure is a great way to ensure that we don't take that treat for granted but that we savor it instead.

Religious groups and philosophers have long advocated for self-denial, whether it's a monthly fast for Muslims during Ramadan, the ascetic life of a Buddhist or the self-denial of Jesuit monks.

By denying yourself something small for a few days, you are exercising your self-control. A skill which can stead you in good stead when it comes to happiness.

What's more, researchers have also shown that if you feel that the time you have available to share with others is limited, you will appreciate that time more.

**Take Action:**

- Identify something that you really enjoy and give it up for a couple of days. Coffee is an easy example. When you next have a cup of coffee, you'll be more aware of the taste and will enjoy the experience that much more.

• Be conscious of how much time is left when you're on holiday or at an event. We often count down the days to the start of a holiday. Try counting down the days left in the holiday.

## Put down your phone

It sounds a bit reactionary to say "put down your phone, it's making you unhappy," -- teenagers would certainly say so -- but there is evidence that links frequent cell phone use and reduced happiness.

Researchers at Kent State University have been exploring the links between cell phone use and various happiness-related factors. Their studies have shown that, "high frequency cell phone users tended to have lower grade point averages (GPA), higher anxiety, and lower satisfaction with life (happiness) relative to their peers who used the cell phone less often."

They have also found links between cell phone use and feeling emotionally close to friends and relatives. While female participants in the study were able to feel closer to friends and family by calling or texting them, male participants experienced no improvement. Both male and female students who used cell phones compulsively or at inappropriate times felt less socially connected to parents and peers. This study seems to show that it's not just how much people use their phones that matters, but how and when as well.

The causal link between cell phone use and happiness is not clear. It may well be that high cell phone use correlates with less time outside and less exposure to sunshine. There also seems to be a link between frequent cell phone use and how much exercise people do. Or it may be that frequent cell phone checkers are already unhappy and are trying to improve how they feel.

Psychologist, David Strayer, has researched people's cell-phone behavior as they drive and has found that when they use a phone, what they notice is cut in half." This has obviously implications when you are driving, but can also impact on your social interactions and your engagement with your environment.

Since we know that being outdoors, enjoying the sunshine, getting exercise and having quality interpersonal relationships are all linked to happiness, it follows that if frequent or inappropriate cell phone use affects these we should take this seriously.

More research needs to be done into this area before any definitive statements can be made about cell phones and happiness, (and shouldn't it be what we're doing on the cell phone, rather than the device itself?) In the meantime, there are a few things you can try.

**Take Action:**

• Pay attention to how much time you spend on your cellphone and what you use it for. Does your cell phone interfere with your interactions with other people? Does your cell phone interfere with your enjoyment of outdoor activities?

• Do an experiment. Give yourself a few hours (or even a day!) without your phone and see how you feel afterwards.

# Conclusion

Thank you again for purchasing this book!

I hope this book was able to help you to develop your happiness skills and so enable you to embrace a more positive attitude. This in turn should help you achieve success.

You've now got a long list of strategies to try out as you seek to make your life happier and more successful.

If you're tempted to pursue happiness relentlessly with your full focus, don't. If you pressurize yourself to be happy, chances are you are not going to meet your own expectations. By all means adopt the attitudes and behaviors that research has linked to happiness but do so in a relaxed and fun way.

The next step after finishing this book is to take what you have learned and put it into action. Choose which happiness strategies you want to employ. Rope in a friend or family member to start some happiness training with you. Enjoy the journey and have fun as you go!


Thank you and good luck

Chloe S